DECORATIVE PAINTING

PAINTING
DECORATIVE
HEIRLOOMS

With DeLane Lange

PAINTING DECORATIVE HEIRLOOMS

With *DeLane Lange*

NORTH LIGHT BOOKS
CINCINNATI, OHIO

About the Artist

DeLane paints the things she loves . . . children, flowers, and the world around her. DeLane's talents have allowed her to explore many diverse avenues of the art world, including teaching tole and decorative painting in the U.S. at many national and regional conventions, Australia, England, and Japan. She also has taught ceramic painting and rosemaling for many years. For the past decade, DeLane has operated a highly successful design company. Her portfolio includes designs for Hallmark Cards, Russell Stover Candy, and the Lily Tulip Company. She continues to design and produce an extensive variety of pattern packets, videos, T-shirts, rubber stamps, and resin kits. Educated at the Kansas City Art Institute, DeLane has always had a need to create. She has combined this creativity with her desire to share her knowledge and be the effective teacher she is today. ❧

03 02 01 00 99   5 4 3 2 1

Library of Congress Cataloging-in-Publication Data

Lange, DeLane
    Painting decorative heirlooms with DeLane Lange / by DeLane Lange.
        p.   cm.
    Includes index.
    ISBN 0-89134-942-1 (alk. paper)—ISBN 0-89134-869-7 (pbk. : alk. paper)
    1. Painting. 2. Painted woodwork. 3. Decoration and ornament—Victorian style. 4. Acrylic painting—Technique. I. Title.
TT385.L332   1999
745.7'23—dc21   98-45644
                                                                                                                        CIP

Editor: Kathryn Kipp and Heather Dakota
Production editor: Nicole R. Klungle
Designer: Angela Lennert Wilcox
Cover designer: Candace Haught
Production coordinator: John L. Peavler

Dedication

I'd like to dedicate this to my husband and my oldest daughter, Kim. Don is my inspiration, support, and my spiritual guide. The hands-on, hard-working, spell-checking, brain-racking other part of this team is Kim! She smoothes the paths and assists in our everyday business and still worked so hard on this book. It will be our accomplishment, not just mine.

Acknowledgments

I would like to acknowledge the people who deserve special thanks, and without whom this book would not have been possible. To Rosemary Reynolds and DecoArt for the best paint in the world and the fastest service! To Gus Dovellos of Royal/Langnickel for his generosity and wonderful brushes. A special thank you to my woodmen for always inspiring me. A very big thank you goes to the kind and hospitable people at North Light: To Greg Albert for all his hard work and effort during the photo session and the fantastic restaurants! To Kathy Kipp for her organization and caring efforts. To Heather Dakota and Nicole Klungle for their editing and finishing touches! To Kim, my daughter and executive director, thank you for all your hard work on this book. I couldn't have done it without you. To Donald, my husband, thank you for accompanying me to Cincinnati for the photo shoot and for your words of wisdom.

Table of Contents

Materials
❦ 8 ❧

Basic Terms and Techniques
❦ 10 ❧

What Makes Things Victorian?
❦ 14 ❧

PROJECT 1

Heart Plaque
❦ 16 ❧

PROJECT 2

Victorian Birdhouse
❦ 24 ❧

PROJECT 3

Our Family Photo Album
❦ 30 ❧

PROJECT 4

Daisy Mailbox
❦ 36 ❧

PROJECT 5

Flower Gazebo Cookie Jar
❦ 44 ❧

PROJECT 6

"Jesus Loves Me" Plaque
❦ 56 ❧

PROJECT 7

Emily's Cradle

❦ 64 ❧

PROJECT 8

Starry Night Santa

❦ 76 ❧

PROJECT 9

Lindsay With Fur

❦ 86 ❧

PROJECT 10

Angel With Roses

❦ 94 ❧

PROJECT 11

Fruit Doorcrown

❦ 106 ❧

Sources

❦ 126 ❧

PROJECT 12

Bridal Bouquet Box

❦ 116 ❧

Index

❦ 127 ❧

Materials

Specialty Brushes

These are a few of the specialty brushes used in my projects. I love the versatility of the comb brushes for painting beards, hair, animal fur, grass, etc. Having a nice large flat comes in handy for basecoating large areas and for making those wide, soft floats. I also enjoy using rounds, flats and liner brushes, which I mention in the different projects. You will notice most people have their favorite brushes, and I think it's good to invest in those. I frequently use a no. 3 round, a no. 8 or no. 10 flat and a no. 1 liner. I usually tell my students to use the brushes they are most comfortable with—people grow into larger brushes as they feel more confident. I have listed several brushes you may wish to use in the materials lists for each project. I really love Royal/Langnickel brushes because they are easy to clean up and they hold their shape well. I also like the fact they can hold a lot of water or paint when needed to give a nice progression of color.

Brushes

These are the brushes I use on a regular basis. They're called "Sunburst" and they're made by Royal/Langnickel. In the flats (Series 2010), I use nos. 4, 6, 8, 10 and 12. The rounds (Series 2000) include nos. 0, 3 and 5. I also like the 2/0 liner brush and the deerfoot stippler. However, I want to emphasize that you should use the brushes you are comfortable with. As you gain confidence, you may want to include some larger sizes.

General Supplies

These are some basic painting supplies; you will need the starred items for every project in this book. Clockwise from the upper left, they are: a pad of palette paper; *tracing paper; *J.W. Etc. First Step Sealer and *Right Step varnish; finishing wax; a *tack cloth; steel wool (for the wax); *sandpaper (I use sanding squares or sanding ovals, as shown); DeLane's Border Tool (creates even borders); a *stylus; an *Identipen (or other permanent fine-tip pen) for tracing patterns; a ruler; sea sponges; and a water container. You will also need *graphite or transfer paper in white, blue, and gray; and a pencil.

DecoArt Americana Paints

I use DecoArt products for their rich, creamy acrylic colors and great coverage, which is really essential for basecoating. I also appreciate the consistency with which they mix their colors; every time you open a bottle of "Medium Flesh" it will always be the exact same color. This comes in handy when matching colors or teaching a project. I prefer acrylics because they dry so quickly and you can repaint over them immediately. This lends itself to many fun techniques.

Specialty Colors

These three colors are in my Face Painting Technique Kit by DecoArt. There are nine additional colors that give all the colors you need to create faces of all races.

DeLane's Cheek Color is great for lips and cheeks. It gives faces a rosy glow of good health.

DeLane's Dark Flesh is a terrific shading color for most Caucasian, Scandinavian and Asian faces. It's a believable shadow color that defines features without overpowering the darker areas.

DeLane's Deep Shadow is used for the deepest shadow color in faces with "high," intense color. It is very effective and gives a robust healthy glow.

Basic Terms and Techniques

General Instructions

Following are a few suggestions to help you paint these projects. All of these designs were painted in flat, opaque colors, except in a few instances where a wash of color was floated in the shaded and highlighted areas.

Sanding and Sealing

Each piece is sanded, sealed and then sanded again. It is important to sand the second time, because the grain of the wood rises to the surface after it's been sealed. Next, wipe the surface clean with a tack cloth.

Applying the Pattern

Next the pattern is applied. The basecoat is the base color applied to the largest area of the pattern. This should be done with smooth coverage. Then the details of the pattern are reapplied and the smaller areas are painted.

Negative Space

The subject or the foremost object of a painting is called the positive space. The area behind this object is the negative space, which is usually either very dark or very light in color.

Shading and Highlighting

The next step is to float the shading and add the highlights. The linework is next. After the linework is completed, the shading may be deepened and the highlights enhanced (as needed).

Varnishing

After the painting is completed, let the piece dry for a few days. Then varnish with a water-based varnish. For the best results, use at least five coats.

Pickling

This term refers to a weathered, whitish finish given to furniture that allows the grain of the wood to show through. I brush White Lightning by J.W. Etc. over a 4″ × 10″ area and rub with a cloth, repeating until the piece is finished. The advantage of pickling is that no sealing or painting is necessary after the procedure is completed.

Painting Terms and Techniques

Shading and Highlighting With Floated Color

Shading and highlighting using floated color makes a painted piece look three-dimensional. To float color, simply dip a flat brush in water and blot the excess by touching the brush to a paper towel. Some water should remain in the brush. Dip the corner of the brush in the color being used. Stroke it back and forth on your palette until you have a nice progression of color.

Side Load

Dip a flat brush into water. Touch one corner of the brush into paint and work the brush back and forth until a nice progression of color is attained with the darkest shade of color on one side and water on the other.

Double Load

Dip one corner of a flat brush into one color and the other corner into a second color. Work the brush back and forth on your palette until the two colors are blended evenly with a distinct color on each edge.

Drybrush

With a flat brush, pick up a tiny amount of paint and apply lightly. If you pick up too much paint, the painted area will look too solid and heavy. It's safer to pick up too little paint, since you can build up the area with consecutive coats. Drybrushing is beautiful if kept light and wispy.

Dabbing

Hold the brush perpendicular to the surface of the board and make short, stabbing strokes to the surface.

Triple Load

Fill a flat brush with a middle tone of color. Dip one corner of the brush into a light color and the other corner into a darker color. Work the brush back and forth until you have a smooth progression of color from dark to light.

Pull Stroke

Hold your brush in a position to move the stroke toward you. To create hair, use an old, worn-out "sprung" brush loaded lightly.

Basecoat

This term is used for painting an area with smooth, even coverage.

Basic Terms and Techniques

Scumbling

Use a flat brush to paint two short, vertical strokes side by side. Now, overlap the bottom of these two strokes with one short, horizontal stroke. These basic strokes always remain the same, but you will develop your own pattern the more you do this.

Double-Edged Float

Using a large brush and a light-color float, pull the stroke down and lift the brush. Turn the brush over and pull the stroke down with the two color edges meeting. This creates a gentle color change suggesting a highlight. This technique can be used for dark colors, but I prefer using it for highlighting.

Stippling

To achieve a textured effect, use a ''sprung'' brush, stippling brush or a deerfoot. Dip the brush vertically into the paint. Then, depending on the desired effect, pounce or work off some of the pigment on a paper towel. Apply the paint quickly by pouncing the brush up and down, leaving a pattern of dots or marks to add texture on the surface.

Wash

Thin your color with water until it becomes transparent with an inky consistency.

Glazing

Apply an even wash of paint mixed with either Delta Ceramcoat Faux Finish Glaze Base, Extender, Control Medium or water to create a transparent, but not runny, consistency.

Soft Float

Make a special effort to broaden the color progression of a float.

"Check Mark" Technique

These "check marks" are made just the way they sound. A small amount of paint is floated down to the point of the brush and then pulled with the chisel edge of the brush away to form a check mark. A combination of these marks will create ruffles and gathers in fabrics.

Overstroke

Overstrokes are pulled over the top of existing strokes and are usually smaller and a different color than the original strokes.

Spattering

There are special tools for spattering, but my favorite spattering technique uses an old toothbrush and a thumb. Mix a pool of half color and half water. Dip your toothbrush in the paint and spatter by brushing your thumb along the bristles of the toothbrush. You can test the spattering on your palette. If the spatters are too big, add more paint. If they are too small, add more water.

What Makes Things Victorian?

The Victorian Era was named after Queen Victoria. After the untimely death in 1861 of her husband, Prince Albert, she surrounded herself with all the things she loved. Her influence affected everything from furniture to flower gardens to morals. The Victorian Era became a very romantic, exciting and energetic time.

Victoria enjoyed many types of furniture and encouraged craftsmen to combine and embellish the current styles with those of the past to create whimsical and very ornate design styles featuring lace, ribbons and flowers.

In thinking about Victorian art, let's begin with general composition. The seemingly chaotic compositions of the Victorian era were executed in the most feminine way imaginable, commonly incorporating lace, love notes and lavender. The design was usually held together by colorful bits of ribbon or repeated groups of the same flower, and included as much texture as possible. Some favorite Victorian subjects were children, cats, dogs, chickens, flowers (including real pressed flowers), jewels, love notes, pearls, ribbons, Santas and even cottages nestled in the hills.

Colors were as brilliant and diverse as printing would allow in those times. Often, women with time on their hands would embellish printed cards and pictures with embroidery, pressed flowers, spices and ribbons. If a little bit was good, then a lot must be better!

The Victorian era was a glorious, romantic time of plenty, with very ornate furniture and very staid ideas on behavior. In choosing the designs for this book, we incorporated many common Victorian subjects and arranged them with a Victorian feel. These projects will lend a warm, Victorian atmosphere to your home. ❦

Heart Plaque

This wonderful piece of wood is from Oakcreek Woodworks and can be placed anywhere in your home. The wire is shaped with a Victorian flair making this little piece unique. I loved painting the "Battenburg" lace with the delicate pink roses. Even though the piece is very feminine, its message will make anyone smile. I have always loved leaving little messages for my family members throughout my home. I think this makes everyone feel special and gets the day off to a good start.

Materials

General Supplies
sponge brush
basic supplies as discussed on
    page 9

Wood Source
Oakcreek Woodworks

Brushes
Sunburst series 2000 no. 2/0 liner
Sunburst series 2000 no. 0 liner*
Sunburst series 2000 no. 3 round
Sunburst series 2010 no. 4 flat*
Sunburst series 2010 no. 6 flat*
Sunburst series 2010 no. 8 flat
Sunburst series 2010 no. 12 flat
Sunburst series 2010 no. 20 flat*
(*optional)

Palette

True Blue	Blue Chiffon	Napa Red	Hauser Dark Green	Country Blue
Winter Blue	Titanium (Snow) White	Lavender	French Grey/Blue	Taffy Cream
Silver Sage Green	Flesh Tone	Light Cinnamon		

This pattern may be hand-traced or photocopied for personal use only. Enlarge at 132 percent to bring it up to full size.

Basecoat the Surface

First sand the plaque and wipe it clean with a tack cloth. Next, apply J.W. Etc. First Step Sealer with a sponge brush. Let this dry and sand again. (It is important to sand again because the wood grain will rise with the first coat of sealer. For a professional look, the dust and the raised grain need to be removed.) Again, wipe the wood clean with the tack cloth. Now we're ready to basecoat the piece with Blue Chiffon. Two coats will provide good coverage. Let dry well between coats.

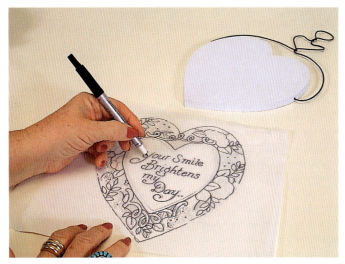

Trace the Pattern

Using a black permanent fine-point pen, trace the pattern onto tracing paper by taping the tracing paper to your work area and then inserting the pattern under the tracing paper. Lifting the tracing paper allows you to check any-time to see if every detail is traced. After the entire design has been transferred to the tracing paper, we're ready to apply the pattern to the plaque.

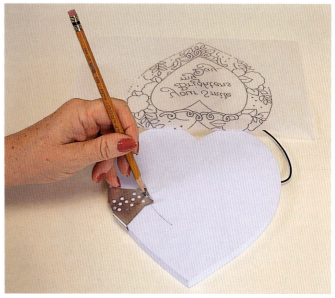

Trace the Border

After the tracing is completed, we will draw the smaller inside heart. The inside heart is drawn by using DeLane's Border Tool and a no. 2 pencil. Insert the pencil in the designated hole to form the heart 1¼" from the outside edge.

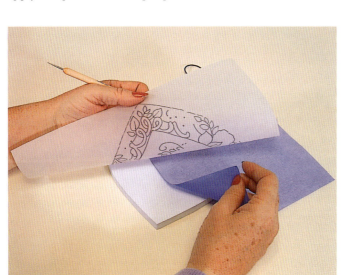

Apply the Pattern

Tape the tracing paper to the wooden plaque so it will be easy to check the pattern as you transfer it. Insert the graphite paper underneath the tracing paper, right side facing down. Using a stylus, begin tracing a small area at the very top. It is important to work top to bottom so you don't forget details. Always check to see if the graph-ite is facing in the right direction.

Check Your Tracing

After transferring, lift the tracing carefully to make sure all of the details have been applied.

Paint the Lace and Center

Paint the Pink Roses

Now we're ready to paint the project. Begin by painting the lace and center heart with Snow White (also called Titanium White). You will need at least two coats of Snow White, or until the coverage is solid. Next, paint the inside section with Winter Blue. Use a no. 2/0 liner brush loaded with Snow White to overstroke the cross-hatched sections.

Practice these roses by following the step-by-step illustration below before actually painting them on your surface. Begin by using a no. 12 flat brush triple-loaded with Flesh Tone, Snow White dipped on one side and Napa Red dipped on the other. Work the brush back and forth on your palette to get a nice progression of color. Next, paint the three back strokes first. Then, paint the three little ones.

Paint the Green Leaves

Now we're ready to add the leaves. Paint the first large green leaves by following the step-by-step instructions using a no. 8 flat brush triple-loaded with Hauser Dark Green, Winter Blue and Country Blue. First load the brush full with Winter Blue. Then dip one corner into the Hauser Dark Green and the other into Country Blue. Work the brush back and forth on your palette to get a smooth progression of color before actually painting the leaves. Now, paint the leaves according to your pattern.

Paint the Smaller Leaves

Paint the smaller leaves with a no. 3 round brush loaded with Silver Sage Green. Complete the leaves by laying the brush down, pulling the stroke and lifting. Refer to the step-by-step illustration below for this technique.

Add the Tiny White Leaves

Paint the last set of leaves with Snow White. Refer to the step-by-step illustration below and paint these leaves according to the pattern.

Add the Blue Blossoms

Next, paint the little blue blossoms with a no. 3 round brush loaded with a mix of mostly Country Blue and a little True Blue. Press down halfway to the ferrule or to the size of the petal you want and then lift the brush.

Add the Purple Blossoms

Continue using the dirty brush from the previous blue blossoms. This means allowing the blue paint to remain in the brush. Add a tiny bit of Lavender to create the purple blossoms. After the petals have dried, add a few dots of Taffy Cream for the centers and shade the centers with Light Cinnamon.

Shade the Center

Float Winter Blue with a no. 12 flat brush inside the center heart. It should be a nice, soft float.

Finish With the Lettering

Transfer the lettering pattern with graphite paper and a stylus and paint using a no. 3 round brush loaded with French Grey/Blue. Let the project dry completely and then varnish with several coats of J.W. Etc. Right Step Satin Varnish. Let the varnish dry well between coats.

Victorian Birdhouse

T his Victorian birdhouse was created by The Cutting Edge in Chino, California. Jim is a very creative woodman who designs beautiful pieces. I love the scrollwork added to this birdhouse. I felt like it should stand out so I decided to paint it white. Sponging blossoms and greenery is fun, quick and very beautiful!

Materials

General Supplies
natural sea wool sponge, small basic supplies as discussed on page 9

Wood Source
The Cutting Edge

Brushes
Sunburst series 2000 no. 00 liner
Sunburst series 2000 no. 1 liner*
Sunburst series 2000 no. 3 round
Sunburst series 2010 no. 4 flat*
Sunburst series 2010 no. 6 flat
Sunburst series 2010 no. 8 flat*
Sunburst series 2050 no. 2/0 liner*
small stippling brush*
(*optional)

Palette

Titanium (Snow) White	Mauve	French Mauve	Jade Green	Evergreen
Lamp (Ebony) Black	Cadmium Yellow	Hauser Medium Green	Berry Red	Baby Blue
Cadmium Orange				

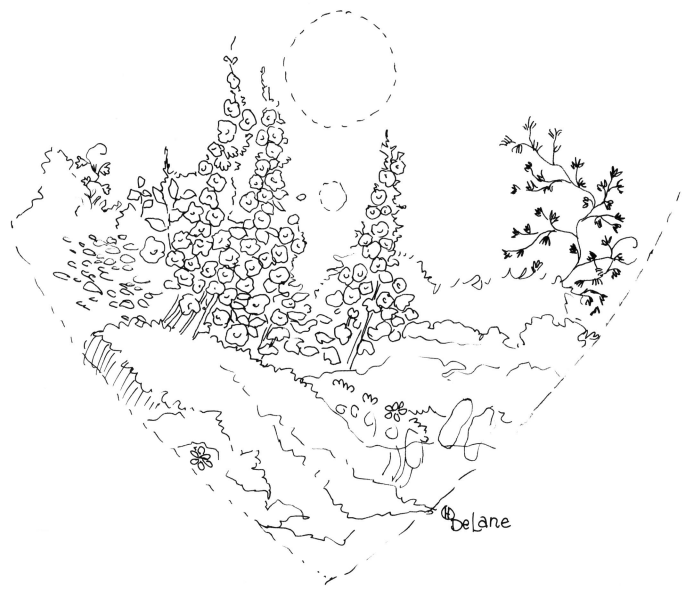

This pattern may be hand-traced or
photocopied for personal use only.
Enlarge to 112 percent to bring it up
to full size.

Basecoat the Surface and Apply the Pattern

Apply the pattern to a prepared surface. Sand, seal (using J.W. Etc. First Step Sealer) and sand the surface again. Wipe the surface clean with a tack cloth. Basecoat the birdhouse with Mauve and the roof with French Mauve. Sponge the roof with Mauve. Basecoat the trim and scrollwork with Snow White. With a stylus, graphite paper and the traced pattern, transfer the pattern onto the wood surface.

Check the Pattern Transfer

Carefully lift the graphite paper and check to see if the tracing was transferred completely before you remove the pattern.

Sponge the Greenery

Begin by loading a natural sea wool sponge with Evergreen and sponge the hollyhock greenery to the left, the middle greenery, and the greenery that goes down on the left side. Then sponge a little Evergreen mixed with Ebony Black (also called Lamp Black) onto the greenery to deepen those areas.

Sponge the Lightest Greenery

Sponge Evergreen mixed with Cadmium Yellow under the hollyhock greenery on the left.

Sponge the Medium Green

Begin sponging Hauser Medium Green on the right side under the hollyhock greenery.

Sponge the Cadmium Yellow

Sponge Cadmium Yellow over the established greenery on the left side, overlapping the Hauser Medium Green slightly on the right side.

Sponge Evergreen, Berry Red and Snow White

Sponge some Evergreen under the hollyhock greenery and down the middle. Deepen these areas with a mix of Evergreen and Ebony Black. Clean the sponge. Reload the sponge with Snow White. On the right and on the left side down toward the front, sponge the Snow White. Reinforce the area in the lower left corner by softly sponging a mix of Snow White plus Baby Blue. Next, sponge Berry Red down the middle and to the right.

Sponge White, Red and Yellow

Sponge a little Snow White mixed with Berry Red on the right side to create a pink patch. Then sponge a little Berry Red on the Cadmium Yellow to create the little orange patch on the right.

Paint the Hollyhocks

Create the pink hollyhocks by mixing Berry Red with Snow White on a no. 3 round. Paint the pink blossoms in irregular shapes. Using a no. 6 flat, shade the blossoms with floats of Berry Red to deepen the color. Add a few Snow White highlights with a no. 00 liner into the middle of the blossoms for the highlights. Paint the yellow hollyhocks the same way using Cadmium Yellow. Deepen a few of the hollyhock blossoms with a little Cadmium Orange. Then add the Snow White highlights into the middle of the blossoms. Complete this project with tiny horizontal strokes of Jade Green around the hollyhocks and a smidgen in the yellow areas. All green linework should be done with a no. 00 liner.

Our
Family

Our Family Photo Album

Creative memory albums are becoming so popular that I wanted to design a cover for those who enjoy painting as well as creating scrapbook pages. I thought it would be fun to make an album for your painting history or for family heirlooms, so I made sure to compose this album cover with lots of Victorian flowers, ribbons and lace. You may paint this on an actual album or on a bristol board that can be inserted into a clear-jacket photo album.

Materials

General Supplies
brown Identipen (or other permanent fine-tip pen)
Krylon 1311
photo album or notebook with a canvas or clear pocket cover
basic supplies as discussed on page 9
tracing paper

Brushes
Sunburst series 2000 no. 3 round
Sunburst series 2010 no. 8 flat
Sunburst series 2010 no. 10 flat
Sunburst series 2010 no. 12 flat
Sunburst series 2050 no. 1 liner
stippling brush

Palette

Toffee	Silver Sage Green	Pink Chiffon	Mink Tan	Sand
Titanium (Snow) White	Colonial Green	Dioxazine Purple	Taffy Cream	Moon Yellow
Sable Brown	Evergreen	Mauve	Antique Mauve	Hauser Medium Green
Light Cinnamon	Violet Haze	Napa Red		

This pattern may be hand-traced or photocopied for personal use only. Enlarge at 117 percent to bring it up to full size.

Apply the Pattern

I painted this project on bristol board basecoated with Silver Sage Green. I planned to insert it into a photo album or notebook with a clear pocket on the cover. You can also do this project on a canvas notebook, in which case you should basecoat the notebook just like the bristol board. Let the canvas surface dry and apply the pattern using graphite paper and a stylus.

Basecoat Lace and Ribbon

Basecoat the lace with a no. 10 flat brush loaded with Toffee and basecoat the ribbon with a no. 10 flat brush loaded with Pink Chiffon. The ribbon base coats will require several layers of paint because the Pink Chiffon is a very sheer color.

Paint the Lace

Using a no. 12 flat brush, float Mink Tan to deepen the ruffles on the lace. The float is done with the "check mark" technique. These checks create the gathers on the ruffles of the lace. Pull the checks in toward the center of the wreath and then outward toward the outside edge. Each one of these gathers creates depth. Create the left highlight with Snow White and the right highlight with Sand loaded on a no. 12 flat brush. To make a scallop around each one of the half circles creating the ruffled edge, float Colonial Green around the outside edge and into the inside edge of the scallops. Use Mink Tan on the handle end of your brush to create the tiny dots around the outside edge of the scallops. Then, with a no. 1 liner brush loaded with Snow White, create the linework, dots and a little flower in the center and outside of each scallop.

Ribbon

Shade the ribbon with Mauve using a no. 8 flat brush, and then highlight with a double edged float of Snow White on a no. 8 flat brush. Also, using a no. 8 flat brush, deepen the shading with a tiny float of Antique Mauve. In order to make the ribbon's loop, darken the point where the ribbon turns over. Then, using a no. 8 flat brush, softly shade first with Mauve and then deepen the shading with Antique Mauve. Next, with a no. 8 flat brush loaded with a small amount of Sable Brown, shade the bottom loop of the ribbon so that it casts a slight shadow. Then, for further shading, float Colonial Green with a no. 8 flat brush underneath the ribbon falling down onto the background. Add little Pink Chiffon dots along the edges of the ribbon to make it look like picot ribbon. This is done by using the handle end of the brush or stylus. These little dots make the piece nice and light.

Basecoat the Blossoms

Basecoat the blossoms with a no. 8 flat brush loaded with the following colors: the rose with Antique Mauve, lilacs with Dioxazine Purple, the narcissus with Snow White and the center of the narcissus with Taffy Cream. Basecoat the daisies with a no. 3 round brush loaded with Moon Yellow. Basecoat the daisy centers with a no. 3 round brush loaded with Sable Brown. Basecoat all of the greenery with a no. 3 round brush loaded with Evergreen. Reapply the pattern details.

With a no. 8 flat brush, create the narcissus petals with a soft float of Hauser Medium Green between the petals. Also use a no. 8 flat brush to highlight the petals with floats of Snow White. Deepen the petals and define the center, using a no. 8 flat brush loaded with Light Cinnamon. Using a no. 10 flat, float a bit of Moon Yellow onto the left-hand side of the narcissus center and then apply a very light wash of Antique Mauve. Next, use a no. 1 liner brush loaded with Light Cinnamon to create an "X" in the center. Create the darkness in the narcissus leaves with a no. 8 flat brush loaded with a float of Dioxazine Purple. Using a no. 12 flat brush, float Sable Brown underneath the narcissus.

Paint the Rose

Deepen the rose in the big "C" and little "c" shapes with a float of Napa Red on a no. 12 flat brush. Then, with a no. 12 flat, deepen the rose further with a float of Dioxazine Purple. Highlight the rose with strokes of Pink Chiffon using a no. 3 round brush.

Paint the Lilacs

Create the little blossoms of the lilacs by overstroking Violet Haze using a no. 3 round. Gradually add Snow White to the Violet Haze to lighten the blossoms bit by bit until they are finally as light as you would like them to be.

Create the Little Yellow Blossoms

Paint the centers of the little yellow blossoms with Moon Yellow and Mink Tan. On the bottom edge of the centers, float Sable Brown using a no. 8 flat brush. Use a stippling brush to stipple a bit of Taffy Cream over the Mink Tan centers of the blossoms. Then, pull a little Taffy Cream onto a few of the blossoms using a no. 8 flat brush. Use a bit of Sable Brown to define and separate the petals.

Apply the Finishing Touches

The lettering is first applied using graphite paper and a stylus. To paint and fill in the lettering, use a permanent brown Identipen or a no. 1 liner brush loaded with Sable Brown. Let dry and then spray with Krylon 1311 to seal.

Daisy Mailbox

*T*his unique mailbox will brighten the outside of any home! The creamy yellows and lovely purples are favorites of mine. The color scheme for this project is similar to those developed in the early 1900s by an artist named Prang. The daisies are fun to paint because you can layer as many colors as you like. The stripes are a nice touch, along with the decorative gold latch.

Materials

General Supplies
DeLane's Border Tool
natural sea wool sponge
painter's tape or masking tape
basic supplies as discussed on
   page 9

Wood Source
Ray Hayden

Brushes
Sunburst series 2000 no. 2 round
Sunburst series 2000 no. 3 round
Sunburst series 2000 no. 5 round
Sunburst series 2010 no. 8 flat*
Sunburst series 2010 no. 12 flat*
Sunburst series 2010 no. 20 flat
Sunburst series 2050 no. 2/0 liner*
(*optional)

Palette

Cadmium Yellow	Lavender	Light Cinnamon	DeLane's Deep Shadow	Antique Green
Cadmium Orange	Violet Haze	Yellow Ochre	Lemon Yellow	Evergreen
Soft Black	Taupe	Reindeer Moss Green	Base Flesh	Sand
Payne's Grey	Titanium (Snow) White			

This pattern is shown at full size and may be hand-traced or photocopied for personal use only.

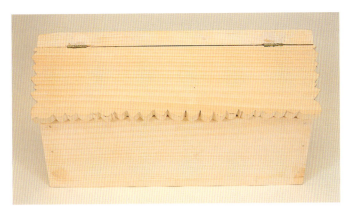

The Raw Surface

Sponge the Stripes

Sponge the Border

Sand and seal the raw surface using J.W. Etc. First Step Sealer. Then sand it again. Basecoat the entire box with Sand. Let it dry. Tape off 1" sections around the mailbox using painter's tape or masking tape. Next, sponge the stripes with Yellow Ochre using a natural sea wool sponge. Let dry and sponge over the Yellow Ochre with Sand to give the piece a textured look. Remove the tape carefully after the stripes have dried.

The border on the lid is made by marking a 1" edge all the way around the lid using a no. 2 pencil and DeLane's Border Tool. Paint the border with Violet Haze. Tap a sea wool sponge into Snow White and lightly sponge over the Violet Haze to help calm down the purple and to give texture to the piece.

Apply the Pattern

Apply the pattern using blue Chaco-paper. This blue paper transfers onto a light surface and makes it easy to see the design. The blue lines will disappear when they come into contact with water.

Check the Pattern Transfer

Lift the pattern and graphite paper carefully and make sure all of the pattern was transferred successfully.

Basecoat the Greenery

Basecoat all of the leaves with Evergreen using a no. 3 round brush and paint the fernlike leaves with Reindeer Moss Green.

Basecoat the Blossoms

Basecoat the top right blossom with Payne's Grey and its center with Taupe. Basecoat the top-left and lower-right blossom with Cadmium Yellow, the top-right half-blossom with Lavender, and the lower-left half-blossom with DeLane's Deep Shadow. Basecoat the centers of the two half-blossoms with Taupe. Paint the half-blossom at the very far left with Lemon Yellow and paint its center with Base Flesh. (Look at the final photo for placement.)

Paint the Individual Blossoms

Reapply the pattern with the details of all the blossoms. Begin painting the individual blossoms according to the following directions: Basecoat all of the centers again with Yellow Ochre. Use a no. 2, 3 or 5 round brush depending on the size of the blossoms.

Overstroke the Payne's Grey blossom on each petal with Lavender mixed with Payne's Grey, then Lavender and then a mix of Lavender plus Snow White. Next, float a little Soft Black over the petals. Float Payne's Grey on the tips of the petals. Float the center with Light Cinnamon. Then add some Light Cinnamon dots. On the bottom of the center, float Cadmium Orange. Add additional Cadmium Yellow dots and then the Snow White dots.

Shade the Taupe blossom with a mix of Lavender plus Payne's Grey. Then overstroke the petals with Snow White. Shade the center with Light Cinnamon and deepen with Soft Black. The Snow White dots complete the center on this blossom.

Highlight the Cadmium Yellow blossom with a mix of Lemon Yellow and Snow White and shade with a mix of Cadmium Orange and DeLane's Deep Shadow. Float the center with a mix of Evergreen and a little Soft Black. Complete the center of the yellow blossom with some tiny Snow White dots. The yellow bud is done the same way.

Shade the DeLane's Deep Shadow blossom with a float of Payne's Grey on the petal tips. Then, highlight with Base Flesh. The centers are a float of Cadmium Orange mixed with Cadmium Yellow. Apply the center dot with a mix of Snow White and Light Cinnamon.

Shade the lavender half blossom with Violet Haze. Highlight by overstroking with Snow White.

Shade by floating the Base Flesh blossom with a mix of Cadmium Orange and Light Cinnamon. Overstroke the petals with a mix of Cadmium Yellow and Lemon Yellow. Shade the center with Light Cinnamon and dots of Light Cinnamon around the edges and add a few Soft Black dots to the center bottom. Finally, add Snow White dots to complete the blossom.

Shade the Lemon Yellow blossom with Yellow Ochre. Deepen the shading with a float of Light Cinnamon. The center is Light Cinnamon and a few Snow White dots.

Daisy Worksheet

Paint the Leaves

Using a no. 20 flat brush, wash the leaves with a mix of light glaze medium and Evergreen behind the composition. Outline the fernlike leaves with Evergreen and shade top edge leaves with a mix of Evergreen and a tiny bit of Soft Black. With a mix of Reindeer Moss Green and Antique Green, emphasize the positive shapes on each leaf by shading the negative space between the veins.

Outline the Blossom Petals and the Tiny White Blossoms

Using a liner brush loaded with a mix of Snow White and Lavender, outline each of the petals on the Payne's Grey blossom. Do the linework around each petal of the Taupe blossom with a mix of Lavender and Payne's Grey. Paint each petal of the Cadmium Yellow blossom with Snow White. Paint the linework on the DeLane's Deep Shadow blossom with Base Flesh. Outline the petals with Light Cinnamon on the Base Flesh blossom and the petals on the Lemon Yellow blossom with Snow White. To complete, add a few small Snow White blossoms throughout the composition. Let dry and varnish with several coats of J.W. Etc. Right Step Satin Varnish.

Flower Gazebo Cookie Jar

*T*his unique wooden cookie jar would be both lovely and functional in any kitchen or breakfast room. It was designed by Sechtem Woodcrafts with a beautiful Victorian flair. I wanted to paint a path meandering through a Victorian garden with a variety of flowers and colorful bushes. I left the inside unfinished and inserted a Rubbermaid container to hold the goodies. Beware! If you finish the inside, the baked items will take on the flavor of paint!

Materials

General Supplies
sea wool sponge
basic supplies as discussed on
    page 9

Wood Source
Sechtem Woodcrafts

Brushes
Sunburst series 2000 no. 3 round
Sunburst series 2010 no. 8 flat
Sunburst series 2010 no. 10 flat
Sunburst series 2050 no. 1 liner*
small stippling brush or deerfoot
(*optional)

Palette

Titanium (Snow) White	Cadmium Yellow	Violet Haze	Antique Gold	Boysenberry Pink	Olive Green	Yellow Light	Flesh Tone
Hauser Medium Green	Hauser Light Green	Hauser Dark Green	Evergreen	Lamp (Ebony) Black	Ultra Blue Deep	Taffy Cream	Calico Red
Jade Green	Pink Chiffon	Winter Blue	Lemon Yellow	Dioxazine Purple	Toffee	Colonial Green	Silver Sage Green
Sable Brown	Mink Tan	Cadmium Red	Williamsburg Blue				

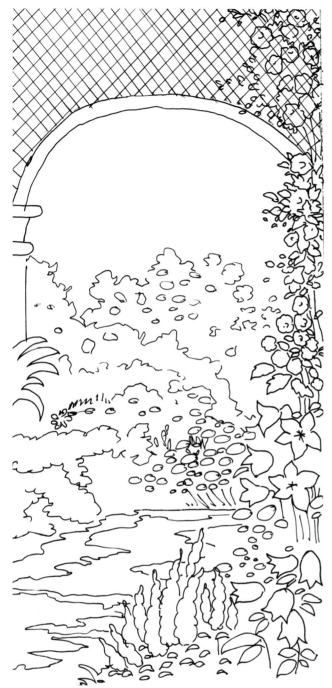

Panel 1 of 6. This pattern may be hand-traced or photocopied for personal use only. Enlarge at 133 percent to bring it up to full size. If pattern does not fill surface, add lattice at top.

Panel 2 of 6. This pattern may be hand-traced or photocopied for personal use only. Enlarge at 133 percent to bring it up to full size.

Panel 3 of 6. This pattern may be hand-traced or photocopied for personal use only. Enlarge at 133 percent to bring it up to full size.

Panel 4 of 6. This pattern may be hand-traced or photocopied for personal use only. Enlarge at 133 percent to bring it up to full size.

Panel 5 of 6. This pattern may be
hand-traced or photocopied for personal use only. Enlarge at 133 percent
to bring it up to full size.

Panel 6 of 6. This pattern may be
hand-traced or photocopied for personal use only. Enlarge at 133 percent
to bring it up to full size.

The Raw Surface

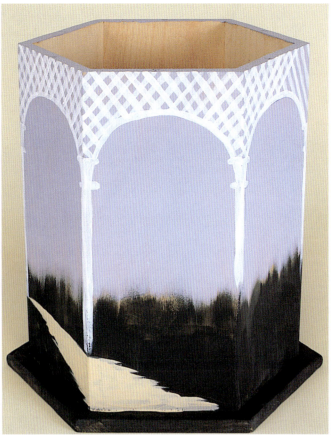

Basecoat the Trellis and Post Pattern

First, sand the wood. Seal the wood using J.W. Etc. First Step Sealer. Then sand again. Apply the basic pattern for basecoating the main areas. Basecoat the area above the grid work with Williamsburg Blue. Basecoat the body of the cookie jar with Winter Blue and the base or the bottom-third of the cookie jar with a mix of Hauser Dark Green and Evergreen. Basecoat the path with Toffee. Using a no. 8 flat brush at the outer edges, float a mix of a little Mink Tan and Sable Brown for the shading on the path. Let dry and apply the pattern of the trellis and post. If the pattern does not fill the gazebo surface to the top, add more lattice. Paint the greenery with a mix of Hauser Dark Green plus Evergreen, brushing upward so the top is irregular.

Basecoat the Trellis

Basecoat all of the trellis linework and the post with Snow White. Using a liner brush loaded with Williamsburg Blue, outline all of the arches and the post. Then float Williamsburg Blue over the arches and post. Then come back and refloat Violet Haze over the arches.

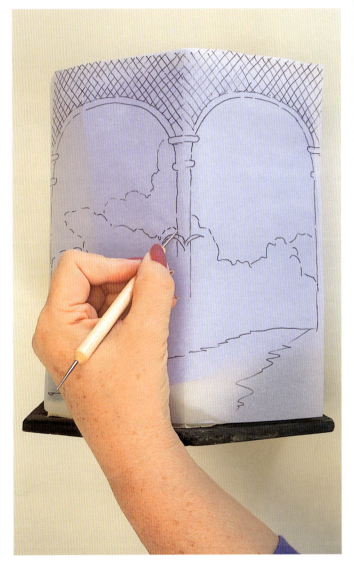

Panel One

Paint the Sky and Bushes

Dance a little Snow White and Winter Blue using a no. 10 flat in a scumbling motion to add interest to the sky. Next, using a natural sea wool sponge, sponge Jade Green to create the bushes above the path. Then add a little Violet Haze into the Jade Green all the way down, almost to the path. Continue using the sponge and add a little Hauser Medium Green and then a little bit of Hauser Light Green as you get closer to the path.

🐝 HINT 🐝 *The bushes are far away and things that are far away are light and bright, but things that are close are dark and dull. We will use this hint throughout this project.* 🐝

Sponge the Bushes

Using a small section of your sponge or a stippling brush, continue applying a little Dioxazine Purple mixed with Snow White into the Jade Green area and into the area near the path. Then sponge Snow White mixed with Violet Haze over the Jade Green close to the path. Switch to a no. 3 round brush and make dabbing strokes horizontally with a mix of Lemon Yellow, Boysenberry Pink, Cadmium Red and a little Antique Gold.

Add the Purple Conical Flowers

For the conical flowers, use a stippling brush loaded with a mix of Dioxazine Purple and Snow White. The bottom should have big sponging and become smaller in the middle; the top should be smallest.

Add the Tulips

Paint the tulips with two strokes using a no. 3 round brush loaded with Boysenberry Pink plus Snow White. By mixing the two colors you'll get various shades of pink.

Add the Lilies and Roses

Paint the lilies with a no. 3 round brush loaded with Taffy Cream, making small strokes from the center out. Come back with Antique Gold lines and dots for the centers. Paint the roses with Taffy Cream, using irregular shapes. Add Antique Gold for the centers. This gives some definition and depth to the roses. Let dry. With a flat brush, create a thin wash of a little Lemon Yellow on some of the roses to give more variation of color.

Add the Stems and Greenery Filler

The filler and stems for the roses and lilies are a mix of Hauser Dark Green and Evergreen on a no. 3 round brush. With this same color mix, continue to fill and pull stems from the bushes, especially where the horizontal dabs of color have been placed. The tulips and conical flowers have Jade Green stems and leaves. I've also added some Hauser Medium Green stems and leaves on the conical flowers closest to the path and a few more above the tulips under the lilies. Also, you'll need to wash a little Hauser Medium Green onto the bottom of the path to provide shading.

Panel Two

Sponge in Some Color

Using a stippling brush, stipple Cadmium Red, then Snow White, and then Cadmium Red again to create an upper middle area that is pink. Then stipple a mix of Dioxazine Purple and Snow White underneath the pink area to the left. Continue sponging Snow White beside the purple area and some down by the pathway. Next, sponge Antique Gold above the bottom white area.

Stroke on the Color

Using a no. 3 round brush, dab Taffy Cream with horizontal strokes under the Antique Gold sponging. Then dab a mix of Boysenberry Pink and Cadmium Red to the area on the left hand corner, next to bottom. Add smaller dabs of Snow White along the bottom, next to the path. Paint the lilies just like the ones in panel one. Using a no. 3 round brush loaded with a mix of Taffy Cream and Antique Gold, paint the centers of the lilies and stamens.

Create the Greenery Filler and Stems

With a mix of Hauser Dark Green plus Evergreen, add bits of grass on the path and throughout the lower part of the composition. There is a large green plant on the right-hand side that has been painted with a no. 3 round brush, using a mix of Hauser Medium Green plus Hauser Dark Green. This plant also falls into panel one in the middle of the post, making the trellis look more believable. Create the filler with a round brush using short dabbing strokes of Evergreen, then a mix of Hauser Dark Green plus Ebony Black. Paint the stems using the same mix, and paint the horizontal leaves with Jade Green on a no. 3 round brush.

Sponge the Greenery

Sponge the bulk of the greenery with Jade Green and then Violet Haze in the upper areas. Now, sponge Jade Green on top of the Violet Haze again. On the lower area, sponge Jade Green, then some Hauser Medium Green. You are now ready to apply some Snow White and finish by applying some additional Jade Green.

Panel Three

Paint the Background Sponging

In the upper right hand corner, begin very softly sponging a mix of Colonial Green plus Ebony Black. Continue sponging downward using Silver Sage Green, then Jade Green on the darker areas that have already been base-coated with Hauser Medium Green and Hauser Dark Green. Deepen the two green areas with a mix of Evergreen plus Ebony Black and sponge the three yellow areas with Yellow Light. In the two lower yellow areas, add some Snow White to make them slightly lighter.

Paint the Purple and Blue Conical Flowers

Using a stippling brush loaded with Dioxazine Purple, Ultra Blue Deep, and then Snow White, begin stippling, larger at the bottom, getting smaller in the center, and then smallest at the top. These colors will give a nice variation of shades and no two flowers will ever look the same.

Paint the Horizontal Strokes

Using a no. 3 round brush, paint horizontal strokes beginning at the top with Snow White. Then add a mix of Pink Chiffon plus Snow White strokes. In the middle, add a mix of Cadmium Red plus a little Snow White, a mix which will give a nice variety of reds. Continue the strokes underneath the yellow sponging on the right. (These are continued around from panel two.)

Paint the Pink Roses

Paint the roses with irregular shapes of Pink Chiffon deepened in the middle with a mix of Calico Red plus Snow White. Using a no. 3 round brush, create the strokes on the roses with Snow White.

✚ **HINT** ✚ *When painting these roses there are three values—first, paint the lightest pink using a round brush, making an irregular shape each time. Next, come back with a little darker pink, mixed with more red and make a swish to create the center. Finally, add a few strokes of Snow White on top to give the roses a soft look and create the third value. Whenever you use three values, you will have a more complete-looking piece.* ✚

Paint the Greenery Stems and Filler Leaves

We will connect the different flowers with a mix of Evergreen plus Ebony Black using a small liner. Try to make some of the leaves dark against the light background and light against the dark. Pull a few thick leaves onto the middle of the post with Hauser Dark Green and Jade Green. Paint the stems in the middle of the composition with Hauser Medium Green and Hauser Dark Green. At the very bottom on a few of the red blossoms, paint some Jade Green stems. Fill in the roses growing up the left side of the trellis with small leaves using a no. 3 round brush and Hauser Dark Green. Then repeat the step in the deepest areas using a mix of Hauser Dark Green plus a little Ebony Black.

Create the End of the Path

The end of the path enters this panel with a brushstroke of Toffee.

Panel Four

warm the yellow area. Move to the bottom area of yellow sponging and add some Snow White to lighten it.

Paint the Conical Flowers

Paint the blue conical flowers with a stippling brush loaded with a mix of Ultra Blue Deep plus Snow White. Stipple the purple and pink flowers over the light yellow sponging. Create the pink conical flowers with a mix of Pink Chiffon plus a tiny bit of Calico Red. Then add some Snow White for the lightest areas. Create the purple conical flowers using a mix of Dioxazine Purple plus Snow White.

Paint the Blossoms

Paint the pink blossoms in irregular shapes using Pink Chiffon. On the larger blossoms, deepen the middle with a mix of Calico Red plus Snow White. Stroke in the few blossoms at the bottom with a mix of Cadmium Red plus Snow White. Paint the final strokes on these blossoms with Snow White. Add some dabs of Violet Haze throughout the pink stroke blossoms at the bottom. Then come back and add some tiny Snow White dabs along the bottom to complete. This gives this panel some lightness, since we don't have a path to break up the composition.

Paint the Stems and Filler Leaves

Paint the stems with a mix of Hauser Dark Green plus a tiny bit of Ebony Black. Create the filler leaves on this panel with short horizontal strokes of Hauser Medium Green.

Sponge the Winter Blue

Using your sea sponge, sponge a little Winter Blue and a mix of Winter Blue plus Snow White into the first green sponged area to give an illusion of negative space.

Paint the Pink Roses

These roses are carried over and done the same way as indicated for panel three.

Sponge the Background

I felt we needed a place to rest our eyes, so I created a field of flowers. Begin at the top and sponge Silver Sage Green. Then sponge Jade Green working downward. Continue using Olive Green and Jade Green, making the transition into the darker area that was already basecoated. Next, sponge a little Lemon Yellow and Antique Gold to

Panel Five

Sponge the First Background and Apply the Pattern of the Lady

Begin by sponging Jade Green, working downward to the dark area already established. Let dry and very carefully apply the pattern of the lady.

Please note: Two-thirds of this panel will be light and the roses will have more detail, which will bring attention to them and the lady.

Create the Second Background Sponging

Sponge the large rose bush behind the lady with a mix of Hauser Medium Green plus Hauser Dark Green. Then come back and add a little Ebony Black to the Hauser Me-dium and Hauser Dark to deepen some of the areas. Continue working with the dirty sponge, adding some Olive Green, and then some Jade Green. The Jade Green should be applied around the lady's skirt in the middle-ground area. Next, add some Hauser Medium Green with your sponge and work it into the darkest greens at the bottom. Continue sponging Hauser Medium and Hauser Dark Green underneath the lady's dress. Next, sponge Snow White on each side of the lady. Sponge a little Dioxazine Purple for the three little conical flowers. Sponge Hauser Light Green on the bottom left-hand side and continue horizontally with Cadmium Yellow. Then add some Cadmium Red to create an orangish shade. Finally, add a tiny bit of Jade Green.

Paint the Pink Roses

The roses are a mix of Cadmium Red plus Chiffon Pink. Deepen the centers with some Cadmium Red and add some strokes of Snow White and Pink Chiffon using a no. 3 round brush. Using this same color mix, add some blossoms below the lady. The Cadmium Red plus Pink Chiffon blossoms on the left have Cadmium Yellow centers. The Cadmium Red plus Pink Chiffon blossoms on the right are just straight color. Above these blossoms are a few Calico Red plus Snow White blossoms with a deeper mix of red for the center. Next, add some Snow White dabs around and below the lady, next to the path. Make strokes to create the daisies by the lady and down near the path. These daisies also have Cadmium Yellow centers. Create the purple iris-looking blossoms with a mix of Dioxazine Purple plus Snow White. Paint the lighter purple on the top and the darker purple on the bottom.

Paint the Greenery, Stems and Filler Leaves

Paint the rose bush stems and leaves by dabbing a mix of Hauser Dark Green plus Ebony Black. The daisy area has many stems of Hauser Dark Green and Hauser Medium Green. Pull a few blades of grass onto the path. Paint the grass with a no. 3 round brush loaded with a mix of Hauser Dark Green plus a little Ebony Black.

Basecoat the Lady

Basecoat the lady with a no. 3 round brush. Basecoat her hat with a mix of Taffy Cream, Antique Gold and Snow White. Basecoat her dress and hat band with a mix of Cadmium Red plus Snow White. Basecoat her face and arm with Flesh Tone. Reapply the pattern details.

Add the Finishing Touches to the Lady

Outline the hat, hat band, her face, facial features, dress and arm linework with a liner brush loaded with Sable Brown. Her hair is barely showing but is created with Sable Brown also.

pink in the middle. Then come back with some Cadmium Red for the final red sponging, especially under the hollyhocks. Sponge Snow White under the pink sponging, then continue using the dirty sponge and apply some Cadmium Yellow and some Antique Gold. Below the white sponging down to the path, sponge a tiny bit of Hauser Light Green.

Paint the Purple Conical Flowers
The conical flowers are done using a stippling brush and Dioxazine Purple and Snow White. These should be larger at the bottom and get smaller at the top.

Painted Blossoms
The hollyhocks are created with a no. 3 round brush painting Taffy Cream-colored irregular shapes, then deepening the centers with Cadmium Yellow. Add some dabs of Snow White around the hollyhocks to lighten that area. Continue adding these Snow White dabs all the way to the path throughout the entire panel.

Paint the Greenery, Stems and Leaves
The filler leaves on the hollyhocks are produced with no. 3 round loaded with a mix of Hauser Dark Green plus Ebony Black. Using the same dark mix of green, add some stems near the path flowers, pulling some onto the path. The stems and plant leaves on the other side of the path should be very light in color. Paint these stems and leaves with Jade Green and Hauser Medium Green. Pull some of the Hauser Medium Green leaves onto the path as well.

Paint the Cookie Jar Roof Lid
Basecoat the lid with Mink Tan. Using a no. 8 flat brush, make short strokes with Toffee to create the irregular looking shingles. Be sure to make them in an irregular fashion. This will give texture to the roof.

Add the Finishing Touches
On the base of the cookie jar, lightly sponge a mix of Jade Green and Silver Sage Green to make the base look more realistic and blend it into the jar itself. Let dry and varnish with several coats of J.W. Etc. Right Step Satin Varnish.

Panel Six

Sponge the Background
Begin by sponging Jade Green for the background and going up higher on the right-hand side to create the yellow hollyhocks. Sponge a mix of Jade Green plus Hauser Medium Green on the other side of the path, creating a nice patch for the purple conical flowers. Continue sponging a little Hauser Medium Green downward to meet the darker area already established. Continue sponging a little Hauser Medium Green into the middle of the hollyhock area.

Next, sponge Cadmium Red plus Snow White for the

"Jesus Loves Me" Plaque

This darling little wooden cutout was designed by my dear friend and woodman Ray Hayden of Golden City, Missouri. I wanted to design a very soft and very delicate piece with a Victorian angel surrounded by roses. One of my favorite Bible songs that I love to hear children sing is "Jesus Loves Me," so I added this song title to the plaque. It's the perfect size for any place in your home.

Materials

General Supplies
basic supplies as discussed on page 9

Wood Source
Ray Hayden

Brushes
Royal series 730 ¾" comb
Sunburst series 2000 no. 2/0 liner
Sunburst series 2000 no. 3 round
Sunburst series 2010 no. 0 liner*
Sunburst series 2010 no. 4 flat
Sunburst series 2010 no. 6 flat
Sunburst series 2010 no. 8 flat
Sunburst series 2010 no. 12 flat*
Sunburst series 2010 no. 20 flat*
small stippling brush
(*optional)

Palette

Antique White	Sable Brown	Hauser Dark Green	Yellow Ochre	Lamp (Ebony) Black
Hauser Medium Green	Neutral Grey Toning	Mink Tan	Titanium (Snow) White	Jade Green
Mauve	Ice Blue	Light Cinnamon	DeLane's Cheek Color	DeLane's Dark Flesh
Medium Flesh				

This pattern is shown at full size and may be hand-traced or photocopied for personal use only.

Jesus Loves me... this I Know

ⒶDelane

Basecoat the Raw Surface

Sand, seal with J.W. Etc. First Step Sealer and sand again. Use a tack cloth to wipe the surface clean. Basecoat with a large flat brush and two coats of Antique White.

Apply the Basic Pattern

Using graphite paper and a stylus, transfer the pattern to the board. Transfer only the main sections that will be basecoated. There is no need to apply the details at this time.

Basecoat the Angel

Begin by basecoating the halo with a no. 3 round brush loaded with Yellow Ochre. All of the flesh should be basecoated with Medium Flesh. Leave the collar and cuff Antique White. Apply a wash of Mink Tan to the angel's gown and hair. Wash the wings and outside border with Ice Blue.

Stipple the Greenery

Using an old, worn-out brush or stipple brush, stipple on the various greens. Do not clean your brush after each color. Begin with Hauser Medium Green, then apply Jade Green and lastly stipple with Hauser Dark Green. Deepen the darkest areas with a mix of Hauser Dark Green and a little Ebony Black.

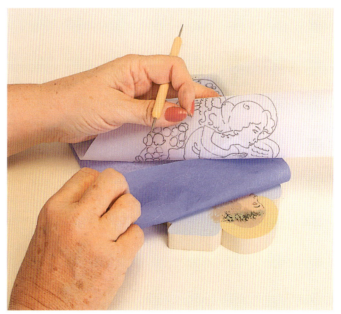

Reapply the Pattern With Details

Now apply all the detail to the project using the graphite paper, a stylus, and the pattern.

Add the Snow White Roses

With Snow White, basecoat all of the irregularly shaped roses.

Shade the Flesh

Begin shading the angel with a no. 6 flat brush loaded with DeLane's Dark Flesh. Create the shading on her hands, in between her fingers, in front of her eye, above her eye on her eyelid and a little behind her nostril cover.

Add the Cheek Color

Float her cheeks using a no. 6 flat brush loaded with a mix of DeLane's Cheek Color plus Medium Flesh. The Medium Flesh will help soften the cheek color. Use the same mix on her lips, with a very soft wash.

Add the Facial Highlights

Using a no. 6 flat brush, float Snow White on top of her nose, on her nostril cover, top and bottom lip, a tiny bit on her nose, down her neck, on her knuckles and a little bit on the right-hand side of each finger.

Paint the Eyes

Paint the angel's eye and lashes with a no. 2/0 liner brush loaded with Ebony Black. The pupil should be Ebony Black with a Jade Green iris. Add a Snow White dot at 10 o'clock with a no. 2/0 liner brush.

Paint the Hair Highlights—First Step and Halo Band

Paint all of her facial linework and the band on the halo with a no. 2/0 liner brush loaded with Light Cinnamon. Then highlight the halo with Snow White. Shade the angel's hair with a dry comb brush loaded with Sable Brown. Using the dry comb brush loaded with Yellow Ochre, add highlights to the curls. Outline and do the hair linework using a small liner brush and Light Cinnamon. Add curls and flyaway hairs too.

Paint the Wings

Using a no. 8 flat brush, begin to float Neutral Grey Toning on the angel's wings next to her face, over her shoulders, under the feathers of each wing and down each of the lines

on the wings. Deepen the shading with floats of Ebony Black in the darkest areas. Highlight the features on the wings with Snow White.

Shade and Highlight the Collar and Cuff

With a no. 8 flat brush, float Ice Blue along the top edges and both sides of the angel's cuff. Also with a no. 8 flat brush, deepen the shading a little further with Neutral Grey Toning. On the edges of the angel's collar and cuff, float a little Snow White.

Add the Dark Green Leaves

Add leaves with a no. 3 round brush loaded first with Jade Green. Then, add some additional leaves using the following colors consecutively: a mix of Hauser Dark Green plus Ebony Black, Hauser Dark Green and finally Hauser Medium Green.

Paint the Dress Details

The darkest areas of the angel's dress should be shaded with a no. 8 flat brush loaded with Sable Brown. The linework on her dress should be Light Cinnamon. Now reemphasize the dark areas with a mix of Light Cinnamon plus Ebony Black.

Shade the top and bottom of the "bowl" of each pink rose with a no. 4 flat brush loaded with Mauve. The top "bowl" is smaller than the bottom. Also, be sure to float the "bowls" in different directions, so they don't look the same.

Deepen the shade with DeLane's Cheek Color. Then add Snow White for the final highlight. Shade the white roses with Neutral Grey Toning in the two "bowls" and with Snow White to create the final highlights. Using the wrong end of the brush, place Snow White dots throughout the roses. Be sure to paint the roses and leaves in the hair also.

Add the Lettering

Do the basic lettering with Mink Tan. With a no. 3 round brush sideloaded with Sable Brown, shade the bottom of each letter. Let the paint dry. Finally, varnish with several coats of J.W. Etc. Right Step Satin Varnish.

Emily's Cradle

*T*his exquisite Victorian-style cradle from *Art Craft Etc.* was designed and painted for my youngest granddaughter Emily. She was such a surprise and blessing in 1994. This idea was inspired by and painted with Mickey Theobald in Redlands, California. We especially like the color combinations.

Materials

General Supplies
DeLane's Border Tool
Delta Light Glaze Base
old toothbrush or spattering tool
basic supplies as discussed on
    page 9

Wood Source
Art Craft Etc.

Brushes
Sunburst series 2000 no. 3 round
Sunburst series 2010 no. 6 flat
Sunburst series 2010 no. 12 flat
Sunburst series 2050 no. 1 liner
stippling brush

Palette

Cadmium Yellow	Jade Green	Light Avocado	Taffy Cream	Pink Chiffon
Taupe	Country Blue	Violet Haze	Boysenberry Pink	Winter Blue
Payne's Grey	Yellow Ochre	Lavender	Summer Lilac	Sea Aqua
Evergreen	Antique Gold	Burnt Sienna	Titanium (Snow) White	

Pattern 1 of 3—Inside the Headboard. This pattern may be hand-traced or photocopied for personal use only. Enlarge at 111 percent to bring it up to full size.

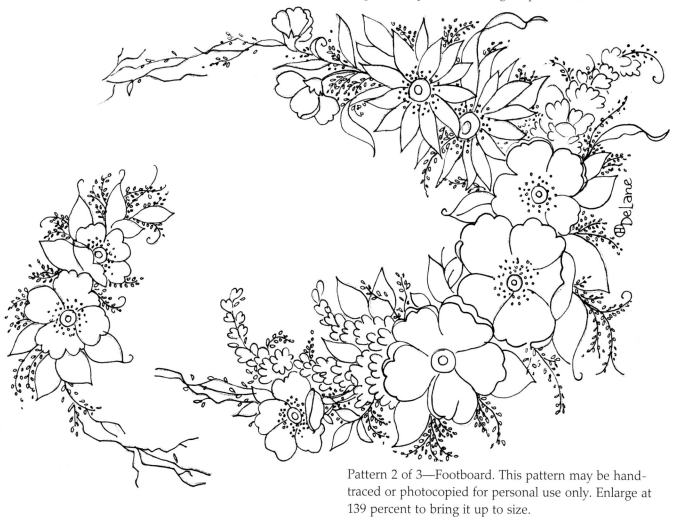

Pattern 2 of 3—Footboard. This pattern may be hand-traced or photocopied for personal use only. Enlarge at 139 percent to bring it up to size.

Pattern 3 of 3—Corners and Center of Sides. This pattern
may be hand-traced or photocopied for personal use
only. Enlarge at 105 percent to bring it up to full size.

Raw Wood

Apply Pink Wash, Basecoat Pattern, and Spatter

Mix equal amounts of Snow White and Violet Haze and wash a thin coat of this mix onto each piece of wood. Spatter with Snow White using a spattering tool or an old, worn-out toothbrush.

Create the Border and Green Glaze

Using DeLane's Border Tool and a pencil, draw a ½" border around all of the pieces. Using a liner brush loaded with Violet Haze, paint the thin, line border. Using Light Avo- cado and Delta's Light Glaze Base, begin glazing the areas behind the leaves and stems.

Basecoat the Blossoms and the Greenery

Basecoat all of the greenery with Light Avocado and Jade Green. The yellow conicals should be basecoated with Antique Gold. Basecoat the two large white blossoms with Winter Blue. Basecoat the small purple blossoms with Taupe mixed with Violet Haze and the two large pink blossoms with Pink Chiffon.

Paint the Yellow Conical Flowers Onto the Headboard

Overstroke the cone with short comma strokes of Yellow Ochre using a no. 3 round brush. Repeat the comma strokes with Taffy Cream overlapping a few strokes and creating some new ones. Add a few tiny bits of Light Avocado to show some greenery in the blossoms. Painting one or two of these flowers will allow a green to show through. Finally, wash the base of these flowers with a no. 12 flat brush loaded with a little Burnt Sienna or Payne's Grey. To add sparkle to a few of the yellow conical flowers, use a no. 12 flat brush and a little Cadmium Yellow glaze.

Using a no. 3 round brush, overstroke with Snow White paint, letting a little bit of the Winter Blue come through. At least one half of each blossom needs to be washed with Boysenberry Pink. Finish by floating a little Payne's Grey around the center and onto the other side of the blossom. Finally, using the no. 3 round brush, overstroke a few of the petals with Snow White for the final highlights. A little Pink Chiffon glaze on the other side of the flower will add warmth. Outline the outside edges with Snow White using a liner brush. This gives the blossom a lacy look. Basecoat the centers with Light Avocado. Basecoat the smaller center circle with Jade Green. Float Sea Aqua on the bottom side. Apply Evergreen and Snow White dots around the edges and some Burnt Sienna dots both close to and away from the centers.

Paint Small Purple Blossoms Onto the Headboard

Float Violet Haze around the outside edges of the centers. Overstroke the petals with Summer Lilac. Glaze Country Blue on half of each blossom and deepen with Lavender. Complete the blossoms with a tiny glaze of Boysenberry Pink and the Payne's Grey, especially where the blossoms overlap. Basecoat the centers with Antique Gold and then float Burnt Sienna onto the bottoms. Next, use a stippling brush or worn-out brush and stipple first with Yellow Ochre and then Taffy Cream.

Finish the Greenery on the Headboard

Basecoat all of the large leaves with Light Avocado using a no. 6 flat brush. Paint the tiny leaves with Light Avocado applied using a no. 1 liner. Deepen the base of each large leaf with a float of Evergreen. Then refloat with Payne's Grey using a no. 6 flat brush. For the very darkest areas, use a liner brush loaded with Evergreen to pull lines out from the base to create veins. Using a no. 6 flat brush, float Jade Green onto one side of each leaf or the tip. A few of these floats should sparkle with a smaller float of Sea Aqua using a no. 6 flat brush. Create the curls on the ends of the leaves with a no. 1 liner loaded with Light Avocado.

Paint the Two Large Pink Blossoms Onto the Headboard

Using a no. 6 flat brush, softly float Boysenberry Pink around the center. With a no. 3 round brush, beginning at the outer tips of the petals, overstroke with long white strokes that end raggedly. Deepen the color using a no. 6 flat brush loaded with a little Boysenberry Pink and then Payne's Grey. Make the centers Antique Gold, stippled with Taffy Cream.

Basecoat the Cradle's Side

Basecoat the flowers using the same instructions as for the headboard.

Shade the Blossoms on the Side

Shade all of the blossoms using the same instructions as for the headboard.

Place Details on the Side

Finish all of the blossoms and greenery using the same instructions as for the headboard.

Finish the sides by adding the deepening floats of Payne's Grey and Boysenberry Pink glazes onto the overlapping flowers.

Paint the Footboard

Paint the footboard using the same instructions as for the headboard.

Headboard Details

Emily's Cradle Assembled

Starry Night Santa

I painted this Victorian Santa on a 16-inch round shaker box by Valhalla Designs. I thought it would be a nice box to hold your Christmas cards. This project would also be nice on a lazy Susan or a door wreath. I particularly enjoyed the scumbling of the various colors for the background. It's not only colorful, but it adds a lot of texture. The various colors added to Santa's beard and fur make this old-time Santa even more Victorian.

Materials

General Supplies
DeLane's Border Tool
basic supplies as discussed on
    page 9

Wood Source
Valhalla Designs

Brushes
Royal series 730 ½″ comb
Royal series 730 ¾″ comb
Sunburst series 2000 no. 1 round
Sunburst series 2000 no. 4 round
Sunburst series 2010 no. 4 flat
Sunburst series 2010 no. 6 flat
Sunburst series 2010 no. 8 flat
Sunburst series 2010 no. 12 flat
Sunburst series 2010 no. 20 flat
Sunburst series 2050 no. 2/0 liner*
Sunburst series 2050 no. 1 liner
(*optional)

Palette

Terra Cotta	Napa Red	Titanium (Snow) White	Antique White	Medium Flesh
Payne's Grey	Boysenberry Pink	Taffy Cream	DeLane's Deep Shadow	Light Cinnamon
Raspberry	Emperor's Gold (Metallic)	Neutral Grey Toning	Yellow Ochre	Moon Yellow
DeLane's Cheek Color	Soft Black	Midnight Blue		

This pattern may be hand-traced or photocopied for personal use only. Enlarge at 182 percent to bring it up to full size.

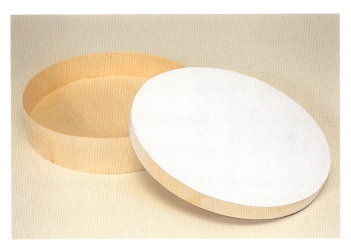

Basecoating the Surface

Sand and seal the raw surface with J.W. Etc. First Step Sealer; then sand again. Wipe the dust off the surface with a tack cloth. Basecoat the top with Snow White.

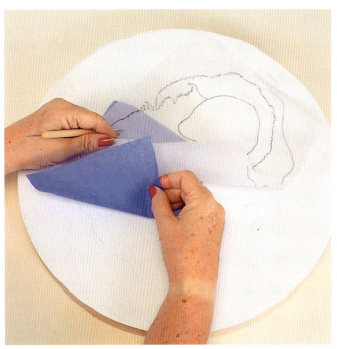

Trace the Pattern

Apply the basic pattern to the lid with blue graphite paper. Carefully lift the pattern and graphite to make sure it transferred correctly.

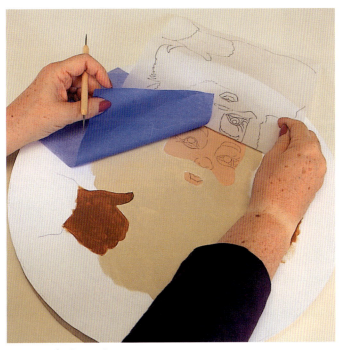

Basecoat the Large Areas

Using a no. 8 flat brush, basecoat Santa's gloves with Terra Cotta. Basecoat his face with Medium Flesh. Basecoat Santa's fur and beard with Antique White. Reapply the pattern details of the facial features.

Outline the Facial Features, Eyeballs and Eyebrows

Basecoat the eyes and eyebrows with Snow White. Outline the facial features with Soft Black.

Scumble the Background

Scumble with a no. 12 flat brush. (Refer to the worksheet below on this technique.) This is a gradual process and you should not clean the brush between colors. Remember that no two backgrounds will be the same and you need to use a lot of paint on the brush because acrylics dry quickly. Begin by loading the brush with Moon Yellow. Work this Moon Yellow around the left-hand side of Santa's face. Then introduce a little Yellow Ochre above Santa's left hand. Quickly work the Yellow Ochre out to the edge. Introduce some Boysenberry Pink near the sleeve.

Finish Scumbling

Using a no. 12 flat brush, work in some Light Cinnamon mixed with Payne's Grey on the left-hand side, underneath Santa's beard and by his face. Float a strong patch of Payne's Grey underneath the hand. Continue scumbling a little Snow White to soften the Payne's Grey. Consecutively use Payne's Grey, Raspberry and Light Cinnamon, working these colors together until you are happy with the color combinations. The Payne's Grey and Light Cinnamon are particularly noticeable toward the bottom of the beard. Come back with Snow White and Payne's Grey, keeping the colors very neutral as you move upward toward the right hand side. Scumble more Raspberry on top of the right hand. Then work in more Payne's Grey. A nice dark area is needed where the Payne's Grey and Light Cinnamon are the predominant colors. Continue working these colors up to the edge of Santa's hat where you should begin introducing the Light Cinnamon, Payne's Grey, Snow White and a little bit of Raspberry. Mesh Payne's Grey and Snow White into the yellow as the colors meet on the other side.

Step-by-Step Scumbling

Shade the Face

Reapply the facial details with your graphite and pattern. Using a no. 12 flat brush, begin floating DeLane's Deep Shadow around the hairline and onto the nose between the nostrils. With the paint-side down, float the wrinkles on Santa's forehead, down the bridge of his nose, underneath his eyes and a little bit above and onto his nose.

Deepen the Shading

Float Light Cinnamon onto the same areas using a no. 12 flat brush; continue around his face, above the eyes, down each side of the bridge of the nose, on the fat pockets, underneath the edges of his cheeks, and on the middle of his nose—but not on his forehead.

Deepen the Shadows

Deepen the shaded areas with a little Soft Black loaded onto a no. 12 flat brush. Float with DeLane's Cheek Color onto the top and bottom of each of Santa's cheeks.

Create the First Highlight

The wrinkle highlights on Santa's forehead are created with floats of Taffy Cream using a no. 12 flat brush. Also, float Taffy Cream above the eyebrow, between the eyebrows and eyes, a little on the fat pockets underneath his eyes and on the centers of his cheeks.

Create the Second Highlight

Reinforce the first highlights using a no. 4 round brush loaded with Snow White.

Finish the Eyes

Basecoat Santa's irises with a no. 4 round brush loaded with Light Cinnamon. Paint the pupils and eyelashes Soft Black. Highlight in Santa's eyes, using just a small comma stroke, with a no. 1 liner brush loaded with Emperor's Gold.

Sharpen the Highlights

Using Snow White and a no. 1 round brush, add the final highlights to his eyes, cheeks, nose and lips.

Shade the Nose, Cheeks and Lips

Using a no. 20 flat brush, deepen the shading on the nose, cheeks and lips with a float of Boysenberry Pink. If you want to give Santa a cooler look, just add a light wash of Payne's Grey on the nose, cheeks and lips. Paint the lips in the same manner with a float of DeLane's Cheek Color and then deepen with a float of Boysenberry.

Shade the Fur and Beard

Begin establishing the shaded areas on the bottom half of Santa's beard and his eyebrows with a no. 20 flat brush and floats of Neutral Grey Toning. Add a little Light Cinnamon underneath his nose, mustache, and the rest of the beard.

Apply Snow White to Fur and Beard

Using a comb brush, apply Snow White in light, fluffy strokes. Allow the Payne's Grey and Antique White to show through on the eyebrows, mustache, fur and beard.

Paint the Flyaway Hairs

Using a no. 1 round brush loaded with Snow White, stroke the flyaway hairs.

Add Additional Colors

Using a no. 20 flat brush, float Payne's Grey to separate the locks of hair and shade around Santa's left hand, underneath his mustache and shade the one lock sticking out from his hat. Next, deepen the curl on the left and the beard using Soft Black. Then float a little Yellow Ochre and Boysenberry Pink on his beard to make it more interesting.

Paint the Hat and Arm

Basecoat Santa's hat with a no. 12 flat brush loaded with Napa Red. The hat stops where it goes to the stars on his right hand. On his left arm, using a dirty brush and the following colors consecutively, use a little Napa Red, Boysenberry Pink, and a little Raspberry to make the arm move forward. Create the wrinkles in Santa's hat with Raspberry strokes and Raspberry mixed with Snow White for the highlights. Use Snow White floats for the final highlights.

Paint the Gloves

The right glove has a negative space which is created using a no. 12 flat brush loaded with Soft Black. Shade the gloves with Light Cinnamon and highlight with Yellow Ochre. There is a tiny bit of Snow White on the tip of the left hand thumb and on the top knuckle, but none on the right—just a Yellow Ochre highlight.

Paint the Stars

Paint the big stars with a no. 6 or 8 flat brush loaded with Emperor's Gold and outlined with Light Cinnamon. Then, float some Light Cinnamon on one side of the little triangles on the connecting stars. Paint the outside edges of the box with Midnight Blue and Boysenberry Pink using DeLane's Border Tool. Paint the border line with a liner brush loaded with Boysenberry Pink to complete. The bottom of the box is painted with Payne's Grey. You can also add stars or scumble the bottom and then add stars.

Lindsay With Fur

*T*his little girl is named after my eleven-year-old granddaughter, Lindsay. I love seeing her in the wintertime with her fur hat. It enhances her lovely face, and those flashing cinnamon-brown eyes are just like her great-grandma's!

I wanted to paint "Lindsay With Fur" on an unusually shaped shaker box. This box by Valhalla Designs was perfect. I also wanted to paint her with a fur-trimmed hat or muff to create a Victorian style.

Materials

General Supplies
natural sea wool sponge
basic supplies as discussed on
 page 9

Wood Source
Valhalla Designs

Brushes
Royal series 730 ½" comb
Royal series 730 ¾" comb
Sunburst series 2000 no. 3 round
 brush
Sunburst series 2010 no. 8 flat
Sunburst series 2010 no. 12 flat
Sunburst series 2010 no. 20 flat
Sunburst series 2050 no. 2/0 flat*
Sunburst series 2050 no. 1 liner*
(*optional)

Palette

Soft Black	Pumpkin	Lamp (Ebony) Black	Light Cinnamon	Dioxazine Purple
Taffy Cream	Williamsburg Blue	Winter Blue	Payne's Grey	Flesh Tone
Sable Brown	Neutral Grey Toning	Slate Grey	Titanium (Snow) White	DeLane's Dark Flesh
DeLane's Cheek Color	Uniform Blue			

This pattern is shown at full size and
may be hand-traced or photocopied
for personal use only.

The Raw Surface

Apply the Basic Pattern

Using white graphite paper, a stylus and the tracing of the pattern, carefully begin to transfer the pattern.

Check the Tracing

After you transfer the pattern, carefully lift the pattern to check the transfer.

Prepare the Surface

Sand and seal the surface with J.W. Etc. First Step Sealer and then sand again. Basecoat the lid with Williamsburg Blue. Tap a natural sea wool sponge into Williamsburg Blue and sponge over the base coat. Then, with a mix of Williamsburg Blue plus Winter Blue, sponge the surface again. Finally, sponge the outside edges with Payne's Grey.

Basecoat the Face, Hair and Fur

Using a no. 3 round brush, basecoat the face with Flesh Tone. The hair is Sable Brown. Basecoat the fur areas with Neutral Grey Toning.

Reapply the Facial Features and Basecoat the Eyes

Using graphite, the detailed pattern and a stylus, carefully trace all of the facial features. Basecoat each eyesocket with Slate Grey.

Basecoat the Ribbon and Shade the Facial Features

Basecoat the ribbons with Winter Blue. Shade Lindsay's face with a no. 8 flat and with DeLane's Dark Flesh. Shade down both sides of her face, under her hairline and eyebrows, on the nostril covers, the center of the septum, underneath the bottom lip and above her chin.

Paint the Cheeks and Lips

Double load a no. 20 flat brush with Flesh Tone and DeLane's Cheek Color. Using the loaded brush, pull the cheeks from the outside edge of her face into the center. Paint the lips with a mix of Flesh Tone and DeLane's Cheek Color.

First Step: Add Highlights

Use Taffy Cream to highlight above the right eye, between and underneath the eyes, behind the nostril covers, the nostril covers themselves, the end of her nose, across the septum and on her top lip. Then highlight along the bottom edge of the chin.

Second Step: Add Additional Highlights

After the first highlights dry, highlight in the same areas with a no. 12 flat brush loaded with Snow White. This gives a nice sparkle to the highlights.

Paint the Face and Eye Shadows

Using a no. 20 flat brush, float Dioxazine Purple on the right-hand side of her face, above both eyes, coming down into the area under her eyes, and a little on the end of her nose. Using a liner brush loaded with Light Cinnamon, paint Lindsay's eyebrows using perpendicular strokes. Then outline the top and bottom of her eyes. The eyeballs should be painted with Light Cinnamon and then deepened with Ebony Black across the eye. Add a comma stroke of Pumpkin on the bottom of the eye. The whites in her eyes are accomplished with a little Snow White strokework. A dot of Snow White should be added at 10 o'clock to create the sparkle! Complete the eyelashes and eyeliner with Ebony Black using a liner brush.

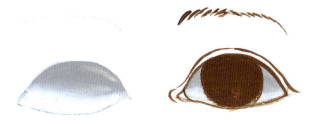

Step-by-Step Eye Worksheet

Paint the Hair and Fur

Using a comb brush, shade the hair with Light Cinnamon. Deepen the shading with a little Soft Black. Paint the first highlights on her hair with Flesh Tone using a comb brush. Then, intensify the highlights with a little Snow White using a comb brush. Brush on the little flyaway hairs with a liner brush loaded with Light Cinnamon.

The white fur should be built up by first using a comb brush loaded with Neutral Grey Toning. Next, clean the brush and reload it with Williamsburg Blue and then finally load the brush with Snow White.

Create Shadows on the Fur

Using a no. 20 flat brush, float Payne's Grey onto the fur next to Lindsay's hair and on the outside edge of the fur on the background.

Finish the Fur

Using a liner brush loaded with Snow White, make some flyaway fur for the finishing touches.

Shade the Winter Blue ribbon with a no. 8 flat brush and a float of Williamsburg Blue. Add a second shading of Uniform Blue. Create the final shading with Payne's Grey. Using a no. 20 flat brush, wash the ribbon here and there with Dioxazine Purple.

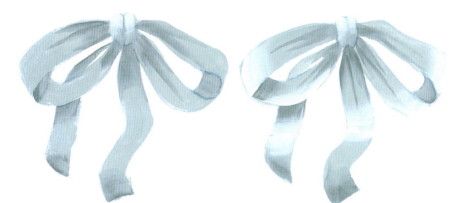

Step-by-Step Ribbon Worksheet

Add the Final Details

To complete this project, add Snow White snowflakes around the lid and shade them with Dioxazine Purple. Let dry and varnish with several coats of J.W. Etc. Right Step Satin Varnish.

Angel With Roses

10

This angel would make a lovely heirloom for any young person. My special angel is Kevin Watkins (1975–1993). Kevin was only with us a short time and was very special to me. He brightened my yearly visits to my dear friend, Jean Watkins, in Thousand Oaks, California. I would like to dedicate this guardian angel to Kevin.

This lovely Valhalla Designs' oval shaker box is not difficult to paint. However, the method of painting is very specific. The colors work well together and the roses and lace give it a definite Victorian feel. I've chosen an angel theme because of its popularity in home decor. You'll be able to use it in your home throughout the year. I hope you enjoy painting this piece as much as I enjoyed designing it.

Materials

General Supplies
DeLane's Border Tool
masking tape
basic supplies as discussed on
    page 9

Wood Source
Valhalla Designs

Brushes
Sunburst series 2000 no. 3 round
Sunburst series 2010 no. 8 flat
Sunburst series 2010 no. 10 flat
Sunburst series 2010 no. 12 flat
Sunburst series 2010 no. 20 flat
Sunburst series 2050 no. 1 liner*
(*optional)

Palette

Payne's Grey	DeLane's Dark Flesh	Dark Chocolate	French Mauve	Light Cinnamon	Mauve	Antique Green	Blue/Grey Mist
Williamsburg Blue	DeLane's Cheek Color	Teal Green	Ice Blue	Sable Brown	Antique Gold	Deep Teal	Hi-Lite Flesh
Lamp (Ebony) Black	Titanium (Snow) White	Neutral Grey Toning	Base Flesh	Glorious Gold	Deep Burgundy		

DeLane

This pattern may be hand-traced or
photocopied for personal use only.
Enlarge at 158 percent to bring it up
to full size.

Preparing the Surface

Begin preparing the surface by sanding and apply J.W. Etc. First Step Sealer. Let dry and sand again. Next, wipe the surface clean with a tack cloth. Basecoat the top of the lid with Payne's Grey. The bottom of the box (not shown completed) should be basecoated with Mauve.

Apply the Pattern

Apply the basic pattern for basecoating purposes with white or gray graphite paper and a stylus. Trace a small section and then check to see if the pattern transferred correctly.

Basecoat the Angel, Stars, Roses and Leaves

Begin by basecoating the areas of the angel's face, neck and hands with Base Flesh. Next, paint a thin wash of Neutral Grey Toning over her wings. Make soft, diagonal strokes of Blue/Grey Mist across the angel's gown. The angel's face, neck and hands need to be basecoated with another coat of Base Flesh and her hair should be basecoated with Sable Brown. Basecoat the star with Antique Gold and the roses and the angel's waistband with Mauve. All of the leaves should be basecoated with Antique Green. Let all dry and reapply the pattern with the details.

Shade the Angel's Flesh

Sideload a no. 12 flat brush with DeLane's Dark Flesh and begin floating this shading color along the back edge of the angel's face, under her cheek, down the back of her neck, around the bodice opening, a little bit in front of her eye, above her eye, a tiny bit behind her nose and in front of her neck.

Create a Soft Float for the Cheeks and Lips

Paint her cheeks with a side load of DeLane's Cheek Color using a no. 12 flat brush. Stroke the brush back and forth on the palette to get a nice progression of color. This will soften the color before you apply it. Paint the angel's lips with a wash of DeLane's Cheek Color.

Using a no. 8 flat brush, float a mix of Hi-Lite Flesh and a tiny bit of Base Flesh above her eyebrows, on the top edge of her cheek, on the bottom edge of her chin, on her forehead, down her nose and above and at the corners of her mouth. Continue highlighting with Snow White on her neck, along her chest and on her hands and fingers.

Paint the Linework on the Face

Paint all of the facial linework with a small liner loaded with Light Cinnamon. Paint her eyebrows, eyes, nose, and mouth. Next, outline her fingers, nails and hands with Light Cinnamon.

Apply Green Washes on the Shadows

Using a no. 10 flat brush, float Teal Green to paint the different shadow areas on the angel's sleeves, next to her hand where the fabric folds, along the bottom of her gown, down both sides of her figure, in all the folds, and the wrinkles of her ruffles.

❧ **HINT** ☞ *Generally, I put the shadows on the right-hand side of the wrinkles on the bottom part of the gown, and on both sides higher on the gown.* ☞

Paint the Highlights on the Gown

Float the first highlight with Ice Blue loaded on a no. 10 flat brush. Pull little ticks or checks on the gathers. Next, float Ice Blue over the gown, covering every light-colored place and along the sleeves and on the bottom of the skirt. When painting a fold, shade one side with a light color and one side with a dark color, back-to-back.

Paint the First Highlight on the Wings

Highlight the angel's wings with a float of Williamsburg Blue in a scallop-like method to create the feathers. It's very important to make the wings look soft. Start the scallops on the bottom and work upward. Be sure not to overlap the scallops. Float Williamsburg Blue on the top edge of the angel's wings and pull strokes to the bottom of her wings.

Deepen the Shadows

Load a no. 10 flat brush with floats of Payne's Grey to deepen the shadow area. Deepen the shadow areas behind the shoulders, down both sides of the gown, under the top edge of the wings, through the waistband, under the right breast, on the left side of the waist and under the right hand.

Paint the Second Highlights

Float the final highlighting onto the angel's right shoulder, the middle front of her gown, the top of her left hip, the top and front of her sleeves, the bottom left side of the top fold and on the first three ruffles of her gown using a no. 10 flat brush loaded with Snow White. Actually, this is just a light float that helps separate the details of the gown.

Paint the Shadows on the Hair

As you examine the pattern, you will notice there are "lumps" of hair. Using a dry comb brush loaded with Dark Chocolate, begin shading each side of the lumps in the angel's hair. Doing each lump separately will create a fantastic effect. Then come back over the Dark Chocolate with Payne's Grey softly so as not to cover all of the Dark Chocolate and do the same with Light Cinnamon.

Paint the Hair Highlights

Highlight the angel's hair with Base Flesh on a dry comb brush. Add this color to each of the hair lumps.

Paint the Second Highlight on the Hair and the Flyaways

Using a dry comb brush and Snow White, lightly highlight a tiny bit on each hair lump to add sparkle. Then do all the flyaway hairs with a small liner brush and Light Cinnamon. The darkest part of the lumps should be shaded with floats of Ebony Black.

Paint the Headband, Waistband and Ring

Paint the angel's headband with a no. 3 round brush loaded with Deep Teal, and use short, wide, diagonal strokes. Create the waistband design by shading with French Mauve in horizontal strokes. The horizontal lines are created behind the French Mauve with Deep Burgundy. Finish the waistband with a little Glorious Gold. Paint the ring with Antique Gold and highlight with linework using Snow White plus Light Cinnamon.

Paint the Decorative Lace and Highlights

Paint the decorative lace design on the angel's sleeves and the bottom of her gown with a small liner brush loaded with Snow White. Next, float a very strong band of Snow White below the design to complete the lace.

Paint the Big Star and Little Stars

Apply the linework on the stars with a small liner brush loaded with Glorious Gold. Shade the left side of each star point section with Payne's Grey. On the other side of the star point, shade with a little Payne's Grey and then come back and place Glorious Gold linework in each one of those sections.

Create the essence of the roses by painting two arcs inside and outside of a "bowl" using Deep Burgundy. Next, deepen the shading in the darkest areas using a no. 8 flat brush loaded with a little Payne's Grey. Highlight comma strokes on each rose with a no. 8 flat brush loaded with French Mauve. Shade the base of each leaf with a no. 8 flat brush loaded with Payne's Grey.

Add the Finishing Touches

This gives us a nice view of the completed top of the lid. Mask off the bottom of the box (not shown here) using one-inch masking tape every 1½" all the way around. Paint the stripes (not taped) with Payne's Grey. After removing the tape, you will have French Mauve and Payne's Grey stripes. Next, intersperse the little stars, starting on the lid or the bottom, with Glorious Gold. Follow the previous star directions to complete. You could add some roses and leaves for flavor or keep it simple with the stripes.

Paint the Gold Trim

Using DeLane's Border Tool and a no. 2 pencil, make a ¼" border all the way around the lid. Using a small liner brush and Glorious Gold, paint the band. Let the paint dry completely and varnish with several coats of J.W. Etc. Right Step Satin Varnish.

Fruit Doorcrown

11

With the beautifully high ceilings of Victorian-style homes, the doorcrown became very popular. Fruit is also a favorite decorative item in Victorian themes. Combining these two popular Victorian styles creates a lovely fruit doorcrown for your home. The ivy border was added because it's become so popular in today's kitchen decor. However, this doorcrown will look lovely in either a dining room or kitchen because the colors are light and clean. This pattern would also be beautiful on a cabinet or in a tiny wall area and would carry on the fruit theme.

Materials

General Supplies
DeLane's Border Tool
old toothbrush or spattering tool
basic supplies as discussed on
   page 9

Wood Source:
Ray Hayden

Brushes
Sunburst series 2010 no. 6 flat
Sunburst series 2010 no. 8 flat
Sunburst series 2010 no. 12 flat
Sunburst series 2010 no. 20 flat*
Sunburst series 2050 no. 2/0 liner
Sunburst series 2050 no. 1 liner*
(*optional)

Palette

Antique White   Deep Burgundy   Dioxazine Purple   Antique Gold   Light Cinnamon   Soft Black   Hauser Medium Green   Yellow Ochre

Boysenberry Pink   Titanium (Snow) White   Hauser Dark Green   Sea Aqua   Jade Green   Hauser Light Green   Napa Red   Williamsburg Blue

Baby Blue

This pattern may be hand-traced or
photocopied for personal use only.
Enlarge at 200 percent and again at
123 percent to bring it up to full size.

The Raw Surface

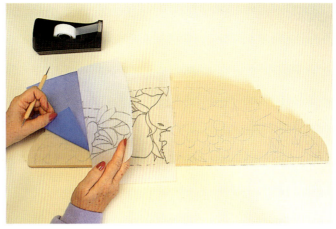

Apply the Pattern

Sand and seal the wood piece using J.W. Etc. First Step Sealer. Then sand it again. Basecoat the entire piece with Antique White. Apply the basic outline of the pattern using graphite paper and a stylus. Be sure to check the transferring to make sure the graphite is facing in the right direction.

Follow the Basecoating Procedure

Using DeLane's Border Tool and a no. 2 pencil, mark off a 1" border beginning on the left and continuing all the way to the bottom right corner. The border does not run along the bottom of the piece. Using a no. 2/0 liner brush, paint the solid line border with Light Cinnamon. Then, basecoat the various fruits with smooth, solid coverage.

Basecoat the cherries and grapes with Deep Burgundy; the peaches and pears with Yellow Ochre; the plums with Dioxazine Purple; and the leaves and stems with Hauser Medium Green. Then, reapply the pattern details.

✁ **HINT** ✁ *You may need several coats of each basecoat color to get good coverage.* ✁

Speckle and Spatter the Pears

Cut the shape of the pears out of a piece of tracing paper. Discard the pear shapes and place the cutout over the pears on the doorcrown. Cover the remaining surface of the entire board (except for the pears). Dip a spattering tool or an old, worn-out toothbrush in thinned Light Cinnamon. Run your thumb through the bristles, causing the paint to spatter onto the pears. This technique will give the illusion of brown spots on the fruit. If necessary, use the Antique White to touch up any spatters you don't want.

Shade and Highlight the Grapes

Begin separating the grapes by adding details with tracing paper. The grapes are shaded with Dioxazine Purple and then redefined with Soft Black for the darkest shading.

Paint the Reflective Light on the Grapes

After each of the grapes has been shaded, float Williamsburg Blue onto the left side. Then, float Baby Blue over the same area. Finally, float Sea Aqua, the strongest reflection, over the other blues.

Paint the First Highlight on the Grapes

With a no. 8 flat brush, float Boysenberry Pink along the bottom right side of each grape to bring it forward.

Paint the Second Highlight on the Grapes

With a no. 8 flat brush, float a mix of Boysenberry Pink plus Snow White to further highlight the grapes.

Paint the Final Highlight on the Grapes

Add a small highlight dot with a small liner brush tipped with the Sea Aqua on the top of the grapes.

Shade and Highlight the Cherries

These cherries are quite dark. The idea will be to highlight and lighten them. Float Boysenberry Pink on the cherries' edges with a no. 6 flat brush. Next, paint a mix of Boysenberry Pink and Snow White on top of the Boysenberry Pink to lighten the outside edges. Then, with a no. 8 flat brush, float Williamsburg Blue on the top edges of the cherries. Create the dark shadows with floats of Dioxazine Purple. These shadows separate and deepen the darkest areas. Create the highlights with Snow White dots on a small liner brush and strategically place the dots to give the cherries a rounded look. With a no. 8 flat brush, paint a wash of Napa Red over each entire cherry.

Shade and Highlight the Pears

Begin by floating a wash of Antique Gold over all the pears. Next, float Napa Red on the left side to create a blush on the pear, and add a little Light Cinnamon to darken the other side. Float a thin, light wash of Hauser Medium Green on the right side, allowing most of the yellow to show through. The rest of the floats are also done with thin washes to allow the spattering to show. Create the highlights with a watered-down mix of Yellow Ochre and Snow White. Next, float Sea Aqua on the bottom of the pears, a little to the left. This will create the reflective light. Float a little Napa Red on the left side of the pears. Next, paint a Boysenberry Pink float at the button end and body of the middle pear. Complete the bottom at the end of the pear with a small liner brush loaded with Soft Black.

Shade and Highlight the Plums

With a no. 6 flat brush, begin floating a mix of Deep Burgundy and Soft Black to shade the bottom and to separate the sections of the plums. Next, highlight with Sea Aqua on the opposite side. Wash Dioxazine Purple over each section to soften them. Then, float Williamsburg Blue on the edges and rehighlight with Snow White mixed with Williamsburg Blue.

Shade and Highlight the Peaches

Using a no. 12 flat brush, deepen the color on the peaches with a wash of Antique Gold and then Light Cinnamon. Next, float thin washes of Napa Red using a comb brush. Highlight over the Napa Red with a little bit of Boysenberry Pink. Continue to highlight with Yellow Ochre and Snow White. In the darkest areas in the middle of the peach, float a little Soft Black. Then, soften the peaches with a wash of Dioxazine Purple.

Paint the Leaves and Stems

Begin by painting a few stems with Light Cinnamon and shading with Soft Black. Deepen the green stems with Hauser Dark Green at each end and where the stem comes out from behind a fruit or leaf. Basecoat the turned-over leaves with Jade Green. Beginning with the grape leaves and using a no. 12 flat brush, float Jade Green down the right side. This shows the sharpness of the edges. Next, float Antique Gold among the veins on the edges and in the middle of the leaves. Float Sea Aqua on the right-hand side of the top two leaves and into the center. Use Soft Black to separate the leaves and to deepen the shaded areas. Next, float Hauser Dark Green underneath the front grape leaves onto the back two grape leaves to separate them from the fruit. With a no. 12 flat brush, float Hauser Light Green along the edges of the long linear leaves. This color is rather bright, so be sure not to use too much! I have brightened some of the other long leaves with floats of Sea Aqua. Darken the center of each leaf with Hauser Dark Green.

❧ **HINT** ❧ *If you want yellow leaves, float Hauser Dark Green over the Soft Black.* ❧

Create the Border

Create the small ivy design with Hauser Medium Green and Hauser Dark Green. Begin with the darker leaves using Hauser Dark Green, then add the Hauser Medium Green to complete.

Complete the Project

Let dry and varnish with several coats of J.W. Etc. Right Step Satin Varnish.

Bridal Bouquet Box

Every bride needs a special place to hold her lovely bouquet and special mementos. What better place than a hand-painted shaker box by Valhalla Designs? I wanted to paint a lasting heirloom for my youngest daughter, Gini, for her special day. Gini loves pastels and lace, as many girls do, so the delicate flowers and lace evolved. When I was planning this lovely Victorian piece, I wanted something she could display as well as a place to put her special keepsakes.

Materials

General Supplies
DeLane's Border Tool
masking tape
basic supplies as discussed on
    page 9

Wood Source
Valhalla Designs

Brushes
Sunburst series 2000 no. 3 round
Sunburst series 2010 no. 8 flat
Sunburst series 2010 no. 12 flat
Sunburst series 2010 no. 20 flat*
Sunburst series 2050 no. 2/0 liner*
small stippling brush*
(*optional)

Palette

| Silver Sage Green | Eggshell | Cadmium Yellow | Baby Pink | Green Mist | Titanium (Snow) White | Hi-Lite Flesh | Napa Red |

| Boysenberry Pink | Terra Cotta | Light Cinnamon | Jade Green | Hauser Light Green | Winter Blue | Lamp (Ebony) Black | Hauser Dark Green |

This pattern may be hand-traced or
photocopied for personal use only.
Enlarge at 150 percent to bring it up
to full size.

Prepare the Raw Surface

The shaker box will need to be sanded, sealed and sanded again using sandpaper, J.W. Etc. First Step Sealer and a tack cloth.

Prepare the Surface

Trace the pattern onto tracing paper using an Identipen. Next, use DeLane's Border Tool to measure two inches from the outside edge and mark a line using a no. 2 pencil. Basecoat the outside edge with Silver Sage Green and the inside oval with Eggshell. Let dry. Position the pattern carefully and tape in place. Insert graphite paper underneath the tracing paper and trace a small section of the pattern using a stylus. Check to make sure the pattern transferred successfully. Then continue tracing the basic pattern without the details.

Basecoat the Flowers and Leaves

Begin floating thin washes of Snow White to make the scallops along the outside edge of the inside oval. Basecoat the two white peonies with Snow White, and the centers with Terra Cotta. Basecoat the top left blossom with Snow White on the top petals and Hi-Lite Flesh on the bottom petals. Basecoat the three other peonies and the peony bud with Hi-Lite Flesh, the ribbon with three coats of Hi-Lite Flesh and the leaves and stems with Jade Green. Deepen the color between the blossoms with Green Mist. Basecoat the coral bells with Hi-Lite Flesh. Reapply the pattern and add the detail.

Paint the Lace

Using a no. 12 flat brush sideloaded with Snow White, go over all the scallops heavily. Do this so the edges are whiter than the inside area. Behind each one of the scallops, float Green Mist on the outside edge of the pattern. Next, use a no. 2 pencil, water and a small liner brush to make a line of Snow White scallops about ¼" inside the larger scallop. Begin by making diagonal lines in each scallop. Make the cross-hatching on all of the scallops in one direction. Then, turn the box around and cross-hatch in the opposite direction. Use the handle end of the brush dipped in Snow White to put dots in the center of each little scallop. Then, with a small liner brush, make the round flowers with four petals and the five-petal flowers

with a dot in the center. Fill in the rest with leaves of tiny comma strokes as noted on the pattern. Add a Snow White dot to the inside tip of each little scallop. Then, in the center of each larger scallop on the outside edge, add a dot. Make another Snow White line above the Green Mist. Add a Snow White sit-down stroke at the top of each scallop. Next, float Green Mist inside each one of the larger scallops and inside each one of the flower petals. Then add a little dot of Green Mist in the centers of the bigger Snow White centers. The little comma strokes are painted with Green Mist also.

❧ **HINT** ❧ *Don't thin the paint too much; you won't be able to see all of your hard work!* ❧

Paint the White Peonies

Reapply the pattern. To separate the petals of the white blossoms and the white area on the two-tone blossom, float Eggshell onto the darkest areas of each petal. Using a no. 12 flat brush, float a little Winter Blue between the petals to separate them further. Next, pull Snow White comma strokes over the petals using a no. 3 round brush. Paint a tiny bit of Cadmium Yellow mixed with Snow White onto some of the petals. Next, paint a tiny bit of Hi-Lite Flesh mixed with Baby Pink on a few petals. Shade the centers using a no. 8 flat brush loaded with a float of Light Cinnamon.

Paint the White Petals on Two-Tone Peony

With a no. 8 flat brush, float Green Mist where the white and pink petals meet, around the center petals and especially at the bottom.

With a no. 12 flat brush loaded with a float of Light Cinnamon, separate the center petals under the "bowl" of the peonies and where the two white peonies meet. Also, float Light Cinnamon where the pink and white peonies meet. This creates an aging effect on petals of the flowers.

❧ **HINT** ❧ *You don't have to separate all the petals completely. It adds a nice variety when they fold in on themselves.* ❧

Paint the Pink Peonies

Begin with a float of Baby Pink loaded on a no. 12 flat brush to create the shadows. Then come back with a float of Winter Blue and shade the bases of the darkest part of the petals. The blue over the soft pink gives a nice lavender color. Then, float a little Winter Blue on the ribbon, too.

Finish the Peonies and Create the Peony Buds

With a no. 12 flat brush, float Napa Red into the deepest shadow areas of all the flowers. Finish with Snow White floats on the tips of all the petals to soften them. The centers should be tiny dots or highlights created with a small liner brush loaded consecutively with Terra Cotta, Cadmium Yellow and a mix of Cadmium Yellow plus Snow White. Deepen further with little dots of Napa Red on the bottom.

Basecoat the top bud of the peonies with Jade Green and shade with Green Mist. Highlight the peony buds with a mix of Snow White and a little Hauser Light Green. Then use Hauser Dark Green for the blossom sepals (leaves of the calyx).

Apply Dark Shading on the Leaves and Stems

Double load a no. 12 flat brush with Jade Green and Snow White. Paint around the outside edges of the leaves. Shade with Green Mist where the leaves go behind another leaf or a blossom. To create the center veins, wash a tiny bit of Hauser Light Green onto the outside edge. Then, float Hauser Dark Green in the darkest areas. Add Green Mist and then Hauser Dark Green to the stems. If needed, soften with a little Light Cinnamon.

Add the Light Leaves and Stems

Float Winter Blue onto the stems. The bottom is mostly Jade Green and Winter Blue.

Paint the Coral Bells

Basecoat the coral bells with Hi-Lite flesh. Add the line-work and shading with Boysenberry Pink and then Napa Red. Be sure to use only Boysenberry Pink thinned with water in various degrees. Use just a little Napa Red to deepen the coral bells. Create the stem work with a small liner brush loaded with Light Cinnamon thinned with water. You can also use a mix of Light Cinnamon and Hauser Dark Green thinned with water.

❧ **HINT** ❧ *What makes this piece so delicately Victorian is the light stems and linework on the coral bells. Be a little shaky with the stems, making them as thin and delicate as possible.* ❧

Paint the Ribbons and Bows

Reapply the pattern detail for the ribbon. With a small liner brush put dots of Hi-Lite Flesh on the edges. This creates a picot ribbon. Using a no. 8 flat brush, shade the ribbon with floats of Boysenberry Pink. Then, deepen the shading with a tiny bit of Winter Blue.

❧ **HINT** ❧ *To create a satiny look for your ribbon, use horizontal floats.* ❧

The Finished Lid

⚘ **HINT** ⚘ *Basecoat the bottom of the box with Hi-Lite Flesh.*
Using masking tape, mark off stripes at any desired width.
Then paint the stripes with Silver Sage Green or a mix of Green
Mist and Snow White. Let the piece dry completely, peel off
the tape and varnish with several coats of J.W. Etc. Right Step
Satin Varnish. To create stripes on a box, always start on the
front of the box. It's easier to make adjustments if necessary. ⚘

Sources

Brushes

Royal Brushes
Gus Dovellos
6949 Kennedy
Hammond, IN 46323
Phone: (219) 845-5666
Fax: (219) 845-4145

Paint

Deco Art Americana
P.O. Box 360
Stanford, KY 40484
Phone: (800) 367-3047
Fax: (606) 365-9739

J.W. Etc.
Jean Watkins
2205 1st Street #103
Simi Valley, CA 93065
Phone: (805) 526-5066
Fax: (805) 526-1297

First Step Sealer

Right Step Satin Varnish

White Lightning

Wood

Art Craft Etc.
415 East 7th
Joplin, MO 64801
Phone: (417) 782-7063

Emily's Cradle

The Cutting Edge
P.O. Box 3000-402
Chino, CA 91708
Phone: (800) 356-8653
Fax: (909) 464-0440

Victorian Birdhouse

Ray Hayden
1208 Clinton
Golden City, MO 64748
Phone: (417) 537-4462

Daisy Mailbox

Fruit Doorcrown

"Jesus Loves Me" Plaque

Oakcreek Woodworks
Rt. 1 Box 156 B
Jane, Missouri 64846
Phone: (800) 477-4434

Heart Plaque

Sechtem Woodcrafts
533 Margaret Street
Russell, Kansas 67665
Phone: (800) 255-4285

Flower Gazebo Cookie Jar

Valhalla Designs
343 Twin Pines Drive
Glendale, OR 97442
Phone: (541) 832-3260
Fax: (541) 832-2424

Angel With Roses

Bridal Bouquet

Lindsay With Fur

Starry Night Santa

Index

Backgrounds, 52-55
  scumbled, 80
Basecoat, 10-11, 109
Basecoating, 33-34, 41-42, 49, 54, 59, 68, 73,
    79, 89, 97, 109, 119
  board, 33
  wood, 18
Birdhouse, 25-29
Board, basecoating, 33
Borders, 19, 39, 68, 105, 109, 115
Boxes, Shaker, 77-85, 87-93, 95-105,
    117-125
Brushes, 8, 17, 25, 31, 37, 45, 57, 65, 77, 87,
    95, 107, 117

Check mark technique, 13, 33
Color palettes, 17, 25, 37, 45, 57, 65, 77, 87,
    95, 107, 117
Colors
  facial, 9 (*See also* Faces)
  floated, 10, 12
Comma stroke, 69, 82
  See also Strokes
Cookie jar, 45-55
Cradle, 65-75

Dabbing, 11
Demonstrations, step-by-step
  Angel With Roses, 95-105
  Bridal Bouquet Box, 117-125
  Daisy Mailbox, 37-43
  Emily's Cradle, 65-75
  Flower Gazebo Cookie Jar, 45-55
  Fruit Doorcrown, 107-115
  Heart Plaque, 17-23
  "Jesus Loves Me" Plaque, 57-63
  Lindsay With Fur, 87-93
  Our Family Photo Album, 31-35
  Starry Night Santa, 77-85
  Victorian Birdhouse, 25-29
Doorcrown, 107-115
Double-edged float, 12
Double load, 11
Drybrush, 11

Faces, 59-60, 79-84, 89-90, 97-99
  colors for, 9
Finishing, 10
  See also Pickling
Floated color, 10, 12

Flowers, 17, 20, 22, 29, 34-35, 37, 41-42, 50-
    55, 60, 63, 69-72, 95-105, 119-123
  See also Subject matter

Glazing, 12, 68, 70

Highlighting, 10

Lettering, 23, 35, 57, 63
Light, reflective, 110, 112
Linework, 10

Mailbox, 37-43
Materials, 8-9, 17, 25, 31, 37, 45, 57, 65, 77,
    87, 95, 107, 117
  sources of, 126
  See also Brushes; Paints

Negative space, 10, 43, 53
  See also Positive space

Overstroke, 13, 42, 69
  See also Strokes

Paints, 9
  See also Color palettes
Palettes. *See* Color palettes
Patterns, 18, 26, 32, 38, 46-48, 58, 66-67, 78,
    88, 96, 108, 118
  applying, 10, 19, 40
  tracing, 19
Photo album cover, 31-35
Pickling, 10
Plaques, 17-23, 57-63
Positive space, 10
  See also Negative space
Pouncing, 12
Pull stroke, 11
  See also Strokes

Sanding, 10
Scumbling, 12, 50, 77
Sealing, 10
Shading, 10
Shadows, 100
Shaker boxes, 77-85, 87-93, 95-105,
    117-125
Side load, 10, 90
Sit-down stroke, 120
  See also Strokes

Soft float, 12
Space. *See* Negative space; Positive space
Spattering, 13, 68, 110
Sponging, 27-28, 39, 50-55
Stippling, 12, 35, 50-53, 59
Stroke(s)
  comma, 69, 82
  -over, 13, 42, 69
  pull, 11
  sit-down, 120
Subject matter
  angel, 57, 59-63, 95-105
  blossoms, 22, 29, 34-35, 41-42, 53, 55,
    69-72 (*See also* Subject matter, flowers)
  borders, 19, 39, 68, 105, 109, 115
  bushes, 50
  clothing, 13, 54, 61-62, 80, 85, 97-104
  coral bells, 119, 123
  daisies, 34, 37, 54
  fabric, 13
  feathers, 101
  flowers, 50, 53, 55, 69, 119-120
  fruit, 107-114
  fur, 84, 89
  girl, young, 87
  gloves, 85
  greenery, 27-28, 34, 41, 49-52, 54-55,
    69, 72
  hair, 83-84, 89, 102-103
  hats, 80, 85
  hollyhocks, 29, 55
  ivy, 115
  lace, 17, 20, 33, 104, 120
  lady, 54
  leaves, 21, 43, 52-55, 62, 72, 97, 105, 114,
    119, 122
  lettering, 23
  lilacs, 35
  lilies, 50-51
  narcissus, 34
  peonies, 119, 121-122
  ribbons, 33-34, 90, 119, 124
  roses, 17, 20, 35, 50, 52, 54, 60, 63,
    95-105
  ruffles, 13, 33
  Santa, 77, 79-85
  sky, 50
  stars, 85, 97, 104-105
  stems, 52-53, 55, 114, 119, 122-123
  stripes, 39, 105, 125

trellis, 49
tulips, 50
Surfaces
  birdhouse, 25-29
  board, 33
  cookie jar, 45-55
  cradle, 65-75
  doorcrown, 107-115
  mailbox, 37-43
  photo album, 31-35

plaques, 17-23, 57-63
Shaker boxes, 77-85, 87-93, 95-105,
  117-125
wood, 18

Techniques, basic, 10-13
  See also Basecoating; Floated color;
    Glazing; Scumbling; Side load; Stippling;
    Strokes; Washes
Texture, creating, 12, 39, 77

Triple load, 11

Values, on roses, 52
Varnishing, 10
Victorian era, described, 14

Washes, 12, 43, 112
Wood, basecoating, 18